Lines by Design Quilts

Lines by Design Quilts

17 Projects Featuring the Innovative Designs of Esch House Quilts

Debbie Grifka

Fons&Porter

CINCINNATI, OHIO

Contents

Introduction

When I'm making a quilt, I'm totally immersed in the process. I forget the details of my everyday life. The designs, the colors and the textures speak to me and we have such fun conversations. I'm happiest when I create every day.

I've been sewing for as long as I can remember. I got my first sewing machine for Christmas when I was seven and began to sew regularly at about twelve or thirteen. Mostly I made tops and skirts for myself, although I also made some full-length skirts for my mother and many of the dresses for our cheerleading team in junior high. I continued making clothes through high school (not so much during college), my early working years and my pregnancies, but I eventually started thinking about quilts, too.

I didn't grow up with any quilts or know anyone who made them. Perhaps it was the 1976 United States Bicentennial celebration that brought them to my attention. Quilts had fascinated and intrigued me for many years before I finally made one.

I was lucky enough to see the Faith and Stephen Brown exhibit of Amish quilts in 2000. Those quilts spoke to my heart. The stunning simplicity of design, the depth of the colors and the beautiful texture of the quilting left me in awe. I did not leave that exhibit thinking that I must make a quilt. In fact, I don't think it occurred to me that I could make an Amish quilt. Finally, in 2002, I began my first quilt and I haven't stopped making them since.

I've completely fallen in love with the process of dreaming, designing and making. The shapes and the colors call to me. I get so excited by all the ideas in my head, I sometimes think, "If only my hands could work as quickly as my brain." But that makes it sound as if I want to rush the process, and it also minimizes the pleasure I take in the making. I'm totally at peace with lots of stitching to do and a good audiobook to keep me company.

So, why lines? I've always loved clean lines in architecture, furniture and clothes. I'm drawn to anything with strong graphic impact that distills a shape to its essence. Lines convey an idea in as few "words" as possible, letting others fill in the details with their own imaginations. Lines offer unlimited potential from bold, straight lines to lush curves and lines that draw pictures.

Whether you make the projects in this book exactly as they appear here or use them as jumping off points for your own exploration of line, I wish you much joy and peace in the making!

Chapter 1

Tools and Techniques

Lots of wonderful and amazing tools are available to help make your quilting life easier. If you are just getting started or, like me, aren't much of a gadget junkie, keeping it simple with just the basic necessities is a great way to go. You can always add to your toolbox later.

This chapter introduces the necessary tools for quilting as well as some of the basic techniques you'll use to make the quilts in this book.

Tools and Supplies

Sewing Machine, Needles and Thread

A good sewing machine is your most important tool. However, it doesn't have to be fancy or new. I sewed on a thirty-year-old Kenmore eight-stitch machine for the first ten years of my quilting life. In 2012, I bought a Janome Horizon 7700. I love my new machine and the things it can do that the old one couldn't, but I made a lot of great quilts on that old one.

The feet I use the most are the utility foot (the basic one that came with the machine), the ¼" (6mm) foot, the open-toed appliqué foot, and the walking foot.

I buy two different sizes of needles for my machine—70 and 80 Microtex sharps. I use the 70s when I piece or appliqué and the 80s when I'm quilting.

Cotton thread is my thread of choice for both piecing and quilting, although I occasionally use polyester if I can't find the color I want in cotton. I usually use Aurifil or Gutermann. Gutermann is readily available in lots of colors at nearby stores and Aurifil 50 weight is nice and fine, and that lets me put lots on my bobbin and helps keep my seams flat. My machine also likes both of these threads. There are some machines that don't do well with certain brands, so use what works.

Cutting Tools

Rotary cutting tools are a must-have for quilting these days. Their speed and accuracy can't be beat! I use a 24" × 36" (61cm × 91.4cm) mat and have five rulers that I use almost daily. I have a 6½" × 24½" (16.5cm × 62.2cm), a 3½" × 12½" (8.9cm × 31.8cm), and three square rulers that are 12½" (31.8cm), 8½" (21.6cm) and 4½" (11.4cm) square. I use my 45mm rotary cutter most of the time, but I like to use a 60mm cutter when I'm trimming my quilts before binding or on the rare occasion when I'm cutting a lot of layers.

I have three pairs of scissors—one for paper, one pair of larger shears (4" [10.2cm] blades) and one pair of medium-sized scissors (2" [5.1cm] blades). I also have a smaller pair that I keep with my handwork kit.

Thimbles

I love my thimble! I have a Roxanne open sided thimble that I bought not long after I started quilting. I use it whenever I do any handwork, including sewing down a binding. In fact, I never hand sew without it. Some people aren't able to adjust to the feel of a thimble, but mine felt like part of me as soon as I started using it. A good thimble can be hard to find, so I feel very lucky that I love mine.

Marking Pencils

So many kinds of marking pencils are on the market; ask people what they like and why, and see if any of their suggestions work for you. My favorite is the Fons & Porter washable graphite pencil. I use it for marking on appliqué and sometimes for marking quilting lines, as well. It sharpens well, stays sharp and washes out like it says it does. Testing a new pencil before using it in your project is always a good idea.

Other Tools

Other tools you'll need are a good iron, a seam ripper, a tape measure and some pins. Bias tape makers, painter's tape, self-threading needles and starch or a starch substitute are useful. I use painter's tape for taping my quilt backing down when I'm basting and for "marking" quilting lines on smaller projects. Self-threading needles are a lifesaver when burying threads on the back of your project. Starch or a starch substitute helps keep your cutting and piecing nice and crisp.

Batting and Fabric

I use 100 percent cotton low-loft batting for my quilts. My favorite is Quilter's Dream Cotton Select, but there are so many kinds available, give a few a try and see what you like best.

Making a quilt takes time. Even a "fast" project takes quite a few hours to complete by the time the fabric is chosen, cut, sewn, quilted and bound. If I'm going to invest that much time in a project, I am also going to invest in top quality quilt shop fabric to make it. When my budget is an issue, I don't buy cheap fabric, I just make fewer projects or focus on using my scraps.

Techniques

Piecing

I start each new project with a new needle and a clean machine. If your machine likes to chew up the edge of your fabric when you're starting to sew, use a scrap and start sewing that first, then sew off it onto your project. When you finish piecing, sew off your project and onto a scrap and you'll be ready to start again (Figure 1).

It is a good idea to check your 1/4" (6mm) seam from time to time. Most quilting projects are designed for a scant 1/4" (6mm) seam. To check your seams, cut two 2" (5.1cm) squares of fabric, sew them together and press. The pieced fabric should measure 3 1/2" (8.9cm) across. If it doesn't, you'll need to adjust your seam allowance. I do this on my machine by moving the needle to the left or right. If you don't have this feature on your machine, a bit of tape on the bed of the machine can help remind you where the edge of your fabric should be.

Most quilters don't backstitch or lockstitch when sewing the parts of their blocks, and I don't either, but I always backstitch or lockstitch when I'm sewing blocks or rows together. A quilt top withstands a lot of handling, from pressing to basting to quilting and I want the edges of my quilt to stay together.

Machine Appliqué

I love appliqué. It gives you complete flexibility over what you put on your quilt and where you put it. There are many ways to do machine appliqué, and I'm convinced there is a way for everyone. If the methods I use don't suit you, please don't give up on appliqué; try several other ways and see what you like best.

Fusible appliqué is one of my favorite ways to appliqué. There are many fusible web products on the market. Fusible appliqué requires a paper-backed fusible web. The one I use most often is Heat 'n Bond Lite. Always read the directions for the type of fusible you have purchased—iron temperatures and length of pressing time vary greatly from brand to brand.

Prewashing the fabric you'll use in a fusible appliqué project is always a good idea. Some of the chemicals used in the "finishing" of fabric can interfere with the ability of the fusible to adhere properly.

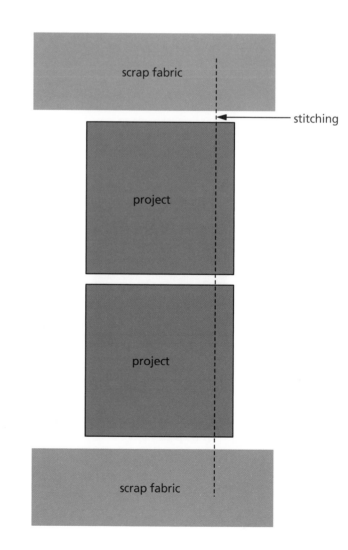

Figure 1

For the same reason, I don't use starch on any of the fabric in a fusible appliqué project.

To use fusible web, trace the appliqué shape onto the paper side of the fusible web, fuse it to the wrong side of the appliqué fabric and then cut out. Then remove the paper side and fuse the shape to the background fabric (Figure 2). This process "flips" the shape from its original orientation, which means the shape must be flipped before being traced in order to appear properly on the quilt. All the shapes in this book are already flipped and ready to trace.

While the fusible web glues the raw edges of the shapes to prevent fraying, I always stitch over the edges as well. There are many different stitch and thread options for this step. I always use thread that matches my appliqué fabric as closely as possible and stitch using a slightly open zigzag stitch (0.5 stitch length on my machine). I like the slightly open zigzag as it keeps the focus on the fabric and not the thread. This is especially true for print fabrics that include more than one color. That being said, I encourage you to make it your own. If you like the idea of contrasting thread for your appliqué or a different stitch, give it a try. Make what you love.

Most of the appliqué stitches will be placed on the appliqué piece, with just a small bit going into the background. The stitches should be perpendicular to the edge of the appliqué shape.

When I pause stitching to adjust the position of the piece, I always stop with my needle in the background fabric. If the next stitch is a bit off, it will show less where the thread and the fabric match.

I like to use a see-through appliqué foot so I can see where I'm stitching. Try to start and stop your appliqué stitches at the same place and avoid stitching over where you started. My favorite way to start and stop is to leave longish thread tails, pull them to the back, knot them and then bury the ends.

Figure 2
Using Fusible Web

Project with appliquéd arrows

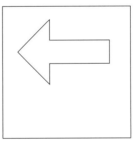 

Trace template onto paper side of fusible

Fuse template to wrong side of appliqué fabric and cut out

Fuse the appliqué to the right side of the background fabric

Bias Appliqué

One of the first classes I took after I started quilting was a bias appliqué class. We made a pretty Celtic block and I loved the process! Soon after, though, I started thinking about what else I could do with these fun strips of fabric. You'll find several ideas in this book.

Bias appliqué is done using strips of fabric cut on the bias of the fabric (a 45-degree angle) instead of across the width (the way fabric is most often cut) or along the length (Figure 3). Bias cuts give the fabric a wonderful stretch that lends itself to flexible and beautiful curves.

Bias tape can be purchased, but it is easy to make, and making your own gives you complete control over fabric choice. My two favorite methods are to use a bias tape maker or what I call the "basting method." In either case, when joining bias strips together always use a bias seam (Figure 4).

Bias Tape Makers

Bias tape makers come in a variety of sizes, the most common ones being ¼" (6mm), ½" (1.3cm) and 1" (2.5cm). A project should specify which size you'll need. If you are designing your own, try a few sizes to see which looks best. Remember that a wider bias tape needs a larger curve to keep it smooth. Making a practice block or two is always a good idea.

There are several brands of bias tape makers on the market. Whichever you choose, just be sure there is a slit-type opening on the top to help you slide the bias strip into the tape maker (Figure 5). Cut strips the width suggested by the manufacturer, then feed the strips into the wide end of the bias tape maker and pull it out through the narrow end. You'll press the tape with an iron as it leaves the bias tape maker; the tip of the iron should almost touch the bias tape maker to get the best result.

If several strips of bias have been sewn together to make a longer strip, it can be tricky to get the seam intersection to go through the bias tape maker smoothly. I often go back afterward, pin near the seam and press again. I also try to avoid joining strips if I don't have to. I'd rather cut a couple of extra strips than deal with lots of seams. If you are working with a design that doesn't need the bias to be continuous, leave the strips in shorter sections if you can.

Figure 3
Types of cuts

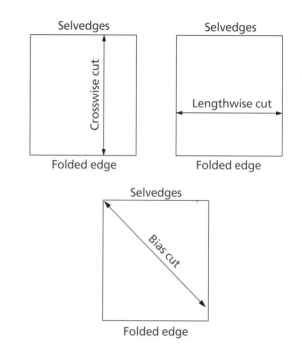

Figure 4
Joining bias strips on a bias seam

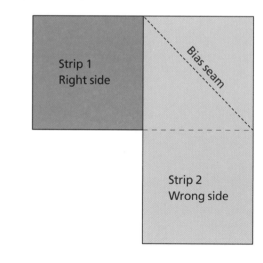

Figure 5
Bias tape maker with slot

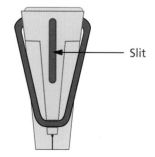

Basting Method

I learned this method from Gwen Marston, an amazingly talented and prolific quiltmaker who probably learned it from one of the many quilters who came before her. I made bias this way for years before I bought a bias tape maker. The advantage of this method is that you can make your bias any width you like instead of just the sizes bias tape makers provide, and you don't need a tool, just fabric, thread and a sewing machine.

For bias that is a generous 1/4" (6mm) wide, I cut my strips 3/4" (19mm) wide. Set your machine for a long basting stitch. Fold the bias approximately in thirds and baste down the center of the strip, taking care not to stretch the bias (Figure 6). Let it feed gently into the machine, folding more as you stitch. Don't fold the raw edges all the way to the opposite side as they can poke out on the quilt when you need to turn corners. If there are seams connecting the bias strips, pin these intersections as you baste.

Do NOT press before you baste. Most likely there will be a few lumps and bumps the first few times you try this method; just remove a few basting stitches and try again. The more you do this, the easier it will be to keep it even.

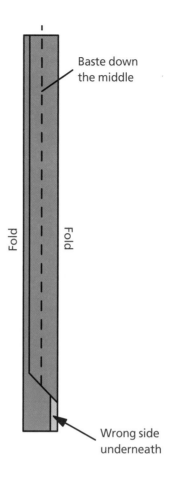

Figure 6
Fold the strip in thirds and baste down the middle. The raw edges do not meet the folded edges.

Pressing Bias Appliqué Blocks

When finishing a bias appliqué block or project, press it face down into a towel on your ironing board. This will preserve the dimension of the bias and allow you to press the background well.

Chapter 2
Pure Lines

From the dramatic repetition of parallel lines in Slats and Bar Chart to the fun of a zigzag in Fault Line and the perennial appeal of the grid in Epicenter, the simple beauty of the line grabs the spotlight every time.

Slats

Finished size: four 16" (40.6cm) pillows

When we bought our current home, all the windows were covered with white metal venetian blinds. While I wasn't enthusiastic about them stylistically, I did appreciate the patterns the light made coming through them at various times of day. Add to these memories my appreciation of the work of Josef and Anni Albers and the idea for the Slats series of pillows developed.

Fabric Requirements & Supplies

Curry: 1 yard (0.9m)

White: $\frac{1}{2}$ yard (0.5m)

Light Gray: $\frac{1}{2}$ yard (0.5m)

Medium Gray: $\frac{1}{8}$ yard (0.1m)

Dark Gray: $\frac{1}{2}$ yard (0.5m)

Batting: (4) 20" (51cm) squares

Backing: (4) 20" (51cm) squares of lightweight fabric such as muslin

Pillow Backs: (4) $16\frac{1}{2}$" × 19" (41.9cm × 48.3cm) pieces

Four 18" (45.7cm) zippers (for pillow backs)

Four 16" (40.6cm) pillow forms

Fabric Note
The fabrics used in this project are Robert Kaufman Kona Cotton Solids in Curry, White, Shadow, Medium Gray and Coal.

Pillow 1

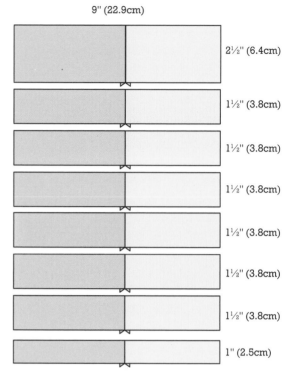

Figure 1

Cutting Instructions

Curry

Cut (1) $4\frac{1}{2}$" × $12\frac{1}{2}$" (11.4cm × 31.8cm) piece.

Cut (1) $4\frac{1}{2}$" × 13" (11.4cm × 33cm) piece.

Light Gray

Cut (1) 5" (12.7cm) × width of fabric (WOF) strip. Subcut (1) 5" × 13" (12.7cm × 33cm) piece. Cut (1) 2" × $12\frac{1}{2}$" (5.1cm × 31.8cm), (1) $1\frac{1}{2}$" × 9" (3.8cm × 22.9cm), and (1) 1" × 9" (2.5cm × 22.9cm) pieces from the remainder of the strip.

Cut (1) $2\frac{1}{2}$" (6.4cm) × WOF strip. Subcut $16\frac{1}{2}$" (41.9cm), $14\frac{1}{2}$" (36.8cm) and 6" (15.2cm) pieces.

Medium Gray

Cut (2) 1" (2.5cm) × WOF strips. Subcut (8) 9" (22.9cm) pieces.

Press seams to the dark fabric.

Step 1: Sew the 5" × 13" (12.7cm × 33cm) light gray and $4\frac{1}{2}$" × 13" (11.4cm × 33cm) curry pieces together on the long sides.

Cross cut (1) 1" (2.5cm), (6) $1\frac{1}{2}$" (3.8cm), and (1) $2\frac{1}{2}$" (6.4cm) pieces (Figure 1).

Step 2: Alternating with 7 of the medium gray pieces, lay out the pieces from Step 1 with the curry on the right and the $2\frac{1}{2}$" (6.4cm) piece at the top, the (6) $1\frac{1}{2}$" (3.8cm) pieces next and the 1" (2.5cm) piece on the bottom. Sew together.

Sew the following pieces to the bottom of this section in this order: 1" × 9" (2.5cm × 22.9cm) light gray; the remaining 1" × 9" (2.5cm × 22.9cm) medium gray; $1\frac{1}{2}$" × 9" (3.8cm × 22.9cm) light gray (Figure 2).

Step 3: Sew the curry $4\frac{1}{2}$" × $12\frac{1}{2}$" (11.4cm × 31.8cm) piece to the light gray 2" × $12\frac{1}{2}$" (5.1cm × 31.8cm) piece. Sew the 6" × $2\frac{1}{2}$" (15.2cm × 6.4cm) light gray piece to the bottom of this section, with the curry on the left.

Sew this unit to the right side of the unit from Step 2 (Figure 3).

Step 4: Sew the $2\frac{1}{2}$" × $14\frac{1}{2}$" (6.4cm × 36.8cm) light gray piece to the left side of the unit from Step 3 and the light gray $16\frac{1}{2}$" × $2\frac{1}{2}$" (41.9cm × 6.4cm) piece to the top of the resulting unit to complete the pillow top (Figure 4).

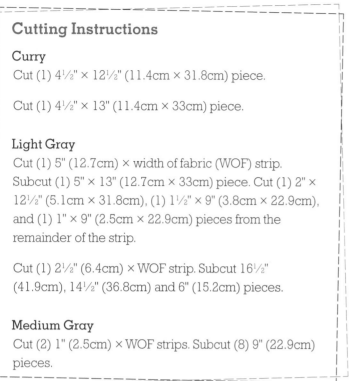

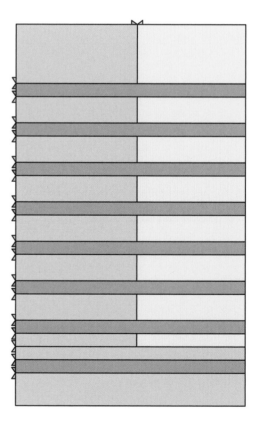

Figure 2

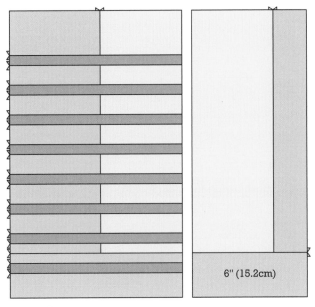

6" (15.2cm)

Figure 3

16½" × 2½"
(41.9cm × 6.4cm)

2½" × 14½"
(6.4cm × 36.8cm)

Figure 4

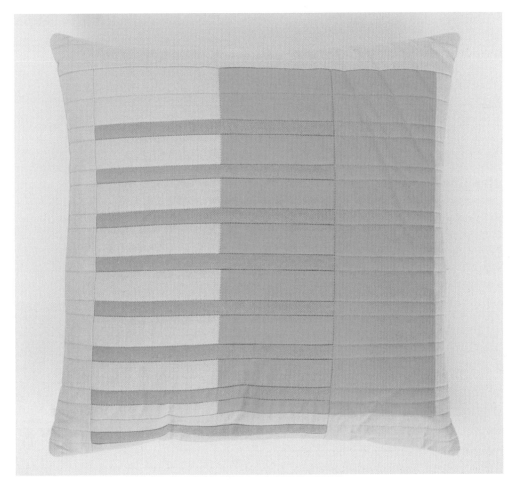

Pillow 1

Cutting Instructions

Curry

Cut (2) 1¼" (3.2cm) × WOF piece.

Cut (1) 2½" × 6" (6.4cm × 15.2cm) piece.

Cut (1) 5½" × 16½" (14cm × 41.9cm) piece.

White

Cut (1) 1¼" (3.2cm) × WOF piece.

Cut (1) 2½" × 3" (2.5cm × 7.6cm) piece.

Cut (1) 3½" × 16½" (8.9cm × 41.9cm) piece.

Dark Gray

Cut (4) 1" (2.5cm) × WOF strips. Subcut (1) 14½" (36.8cm) piece from one of the strips.

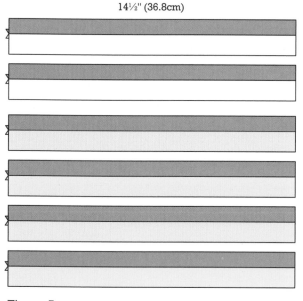

14½" (36.8cm)

Figure 5

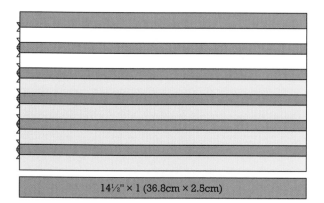

14½" × 1 (36.8cm × 2.5cm)

Figure 6

Step 1: Sew a white and a dark gray WOF strip together on the long edges. Crosscut two 14½" (36.8cm) pieces.

Sew a curry and a dark gray WOF strip together on the long edges. Crosscut two 14½" (36.8cm) pieces. Repeat with 1 more set of curry and dark gray strips to total four 14½" (36.8cm) pieces (Figure 5).

Step 2: With the dark gray on top, and alternating colors, sew the 2 dark gray and white strips together on their long edges. In a similar manner, with the dark gray on top, and alternating colors, sew the 4 dark gray and curry strips together on their long edges.

Step 3: Sew the 2 units from Step 2 together and sew the dark gray 1" × 14½" (2.5cm × 36.8cm) piece to the bottom of this unit (Figure 6).

Step 4: Sew the 2½" × 3" (6.4cm × 7.6cm) white piece and the 2½" × 6" (6.4cm × 15.2cm) curry piece together on the short sides.

Sew this unit to the unit from Step 3, matching the colors (Figure 7).

Step 5: Sew the white 3½" × 16½" (8.9cm × 41.9cm) piece to the top of this unit. Sew the curry 5½" × 16½" (14cm × 41.9cm) piece to the bottom of this unit to complete the pillow top (Figure 8).

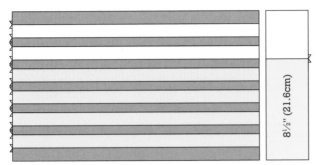

Figure 7

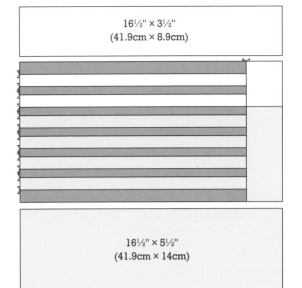

16½" × 3½"
(41.9cm × 8.9cm)

16½" × 5½"
(41.9cm × 14cm)

8½" (21.6cm)

Figure 8

Pillow 2

Cutting Instructions

Curry

Cut (1) 1½" (3.8cm) × WOF piece.

Cut (2) 1" × 5½" (2.5cm × 14cm) piece.

Cut (1) 2½" × 12½" (6.4cm × 31.8cm) piece.

Cut (1) 7" × 12½" (17.8cm × 31.8cm) piece.

White

Cut (1) 4½" (11.4cm) × WOF piece. Subcut (1) 7" (17.8cm) and (1) 5" (12.7cm) piece. From the remainder of the strip, cut (1) 3" × 12½" (7.6cm × 31.8cm); (1) 1½" × 12" (3.8cm × 30.5cm); and 1" × 5½" (2.5cm × 14cm) piece.

Light Gray

Cut (2) 1" (2.5cm) × WOF strips. Set one aside and subcut (1) 12" (30.5cm) piece and (2) 5½" (14cm) from the remaining strip.

Step 1: Sew the white 1½" × 12" (3.8cm × 30.5cm) and the light gray 1" × 12" (2.5cm × 30.5cm) pieces together on the long sides. Crosscut 2 pieces at 5½" (14cm). With the light gray on the left end, and alternating colors, sew the pieces together on the long sides.

Step 2: Sew the white 1" × 5½" (2.5cm × 14cm) and the curry 1" × 5½" (2.5cm × 14cm) pieces together on the long sides. Sew a light gray 1" × 5½" (2.5cm × 14cm) piece to each side of this unit.

Step 3: Sew a light gray 1" (2.5cm) × WOF strip to a curry 1½" (3.8cm) × WOF strip on the long sides. Crosscut (7) 5½" (14cm) pieces. With the curry on the left end, and alternating colors, sew the strips together on the long sides.

Step 4: Sew the units created in the previous steps together as shown in Figure 9. Sew the remaining curry 1" × 5½" (2.5cm × 14cm) piece to the right end of the resulting unit.

Step 5: Sew the white 3" × 12½" (7.6cm × 31.8cm) piece and the curry 2½" × 12½" (6.4cm × 31.8cm) piece together on the long sides with the white on the top and the curry on the bottom. Sew the white 4½" × 5" (11.4cm × 12.7cm) piece to the left end of the unit. Sew this to the section created in Step 4.

Step 6: Sew the white 4½" × 7" (11.4cm × 17.8cm) piece to the curry 12½" × 7" (31.8cm × 17.8cm) piece on the 7" (17.8cm) sides with the white on the left. Sew this to the bottom of the unit from Step 5 to complete the pillow top (Figure 10).

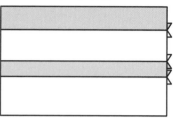

5½" (14cm)

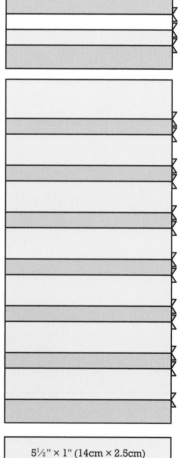

5½" × 1" (14cm × 2.5cm)

Figure 9

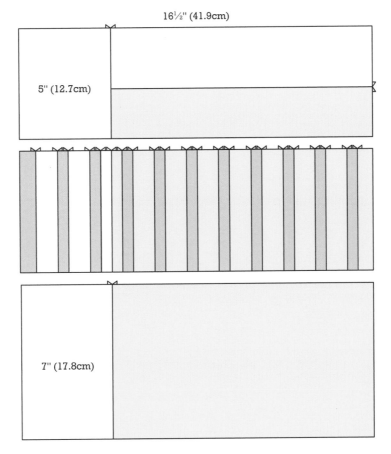

16½" (41.9cm)

5" (12.7cm)

7" (17.8cm)

Figure 10

Pillow 3

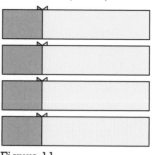

Figure 11

Cutting Instructions

Curry

Cut (1) 5½" (14cm) × WOF strip. Subcut (1) 5" (12.7cm), (1) 6½" (16.5cm) and (1) 11" (27.9cm) piece.

Light Gray

Cut (2) 1" (2.5cm) × WOF strip. Subcut (7) 6½" (15.2cm) pieces.

Dark Gray

Cut (1) 3" (7.6cm) × WOF strip. Subcut (1) 8½" (21.6cm) piece. From the remainder of the strip, cut (1) 2" × 5½" (5.1cm × 14cm), 2" × 13½" (5.1cm × 34.3cm), and (2) 1¼" × 6½" (3.2cm × 16.5cm) pieces.

Cut (1) 4½" (11.4cm) × WOF strip. Subcut (1) 5½" (14cm) piece. From the remainder of the strip, cut (1) 3½" × 6½" (8.9cm × 16.5cm) piece and (1) 3½" × 16½" (8.9cm × 41.9cm) piece.

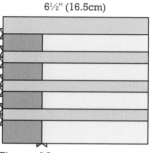

Figure 12

Step 1: Sew the curry 5" × 5½" (12.7cm × 14cm) piece to the dark gray 2" × 5½" (2.5cm × 14cm) piece on the 5½" (14cm) sides. Crosscut this to (4) 1¼" (3.2cm) pieces (Figure 11).

Step 2: Beginning with a light gray 1" × 6½" (2.5cm × 16.5cm) piece and alternating with units from Step 1 (keeping the dark gray on the left side), sew the Step 1 and 4 light gray units together on the long sides (Figure 12).

Step 3: Sew 2 dark gray 1¼" × 6½" (3.2cm × 16.5cm) pieces in between 3 light gray 1" × 6½" (2.5cm × 16.5cm) pieces. Sew this unit to the unit from Step 2, alternating light gray strips (Figure 13).

Sew a curry 6½" × 5½" (16.5cm × 14cm) piece to a dark gray 6½" × 3½" (16.5cm × 8.9cm) piece on the long sides with the curry piece on top. Sew this to the right side of the unit from above.

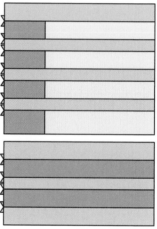

Figure 13

Step 4: Sew a dark gray 3" × 8½" (7.6cm × 21.6cm) piece to the left side of the unit from Step 3 (Figure 14).

Step 5: Sew a dark gray 4½" × 5½" (11.4cm × 14cm) piece to the curry 11" × 5½" (27.9cm × 14cm) piece along the 5½" (14cm) sides with the dark gray on the left. Sew this to the top of the unit from Step 4 (Figure 15).

Step 6: Sew a dark gray 2" × 13½" (5.1cm × 34.3cm) piece to the right side of the unit from above. Sew the dark gray 3½" × 16½" (8.9cm × 41.9cm) piece to the top of this unit to complete the pillow top (Figure 16).

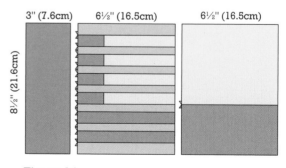

Figure 14

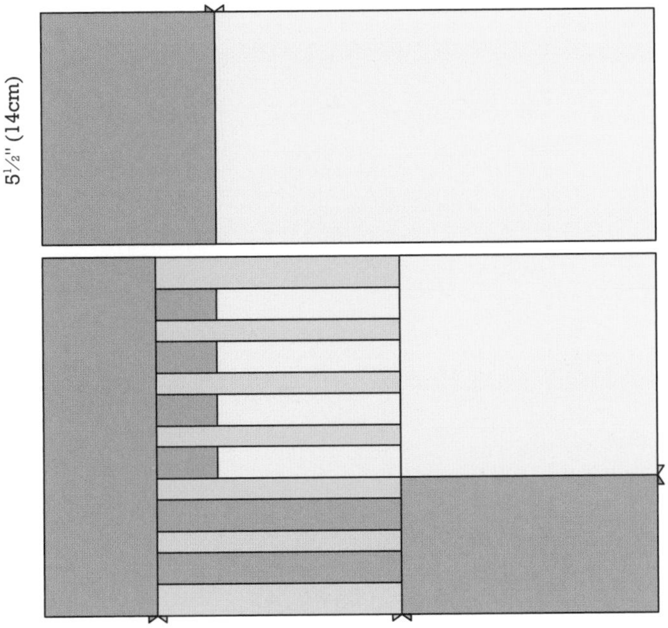

5¹⁄₂" (14cm)

Figure 15

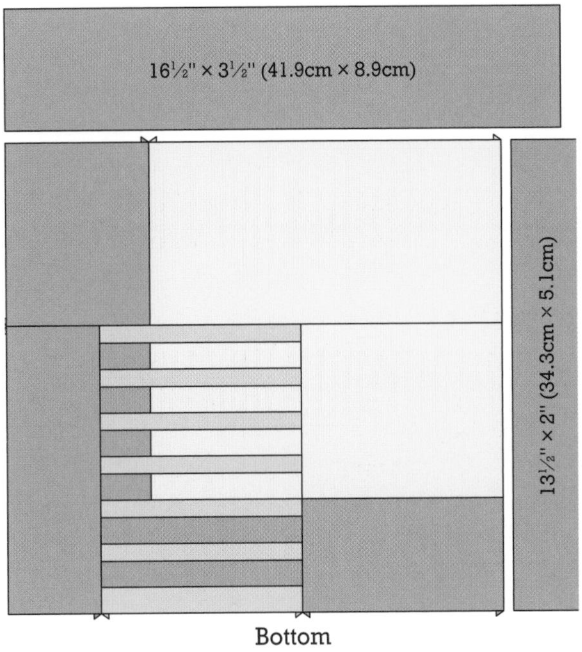

16¹⁄₂" × 3¹⁄₂" (41.9cm × 8.9cm)

13¹⁄₂" × 2" (34.3cm × 5.1cm)

Bottom

Figure 16

Pillow 4

Finishing the Pillows

Step 1: To finish the pillows with a hidden back zipper, cut each 16½" × 19" (41.9cm × 48.3cm) pillow back into 16½" × 7" (41.9cm × 17.8cm) and 16½" × 12" (41.9cm × 30.5cm) sections.

Press under 1¼" (3.2cm) along a 16½" (41.9cm) edge of each 12" (30.5cm) section.

Step 2: Cut (8) 1" × 3" (2.5cm × 7.6cm) pieces from the pillow scraps to make zipper tabs, 2 for each pillow. These will be hidden so color is not important.

Fold the tabs in half; they'll measure 1" × 1½" (2.5cm × 3.8cm). Place the first tab so that the raw edges just cover the bottom zipper stop and the fold is toward the center of the zipper. Stitch along the fold, across the zipper teeth. Open the zipper partway and place the fold of the second tab 13½" (34.3cm) from the first tab (fold again facing the center of the zipper). Pin the sides of the zipper to the tab so they are as close together as possible while still being open. Stitch along the fold across the zipper teeth. Trim the zipper ¼" (6mm) from each stitching line. Repeat with the remaining zippers and tabs.

Step 3: Place the zipper face down (right sides together) and align with the raw edge of the 1¼" (3.2cm) fold of a pillow back piece. Stitch the left side of the zipper in place (Figure 17). Press the fold away from the zipper for now. Repeat with the remaining zippers and pillow back pieces.

Step 4: Place the 16½" × 7" (41.9cm × 17.8cm) pillow back piece right sides together with the piece from Step 3 and stitch the other side of the zipper in place (Figure 18). Press the fold back over the zipper.

Leaving the zipper partway open, place the pillow top and back right sides together. Stitch all the way around the pillow using a ½" (1.3cm) seam. Turn the pillow right side out through the zipper opening. Press and insert a 16" (40.6cm) pillow form. Repeat with the remaining pillows.

Step 5: Layer the pillow fronts with the batting and backing squares, and quilt as desired. The project pillows are quilted with straight lines echoing the piecing.

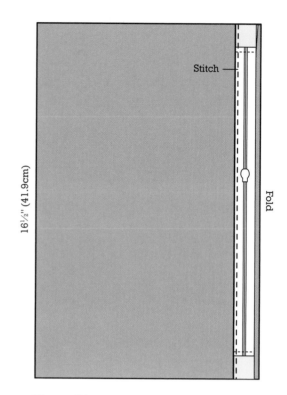

Figure 17

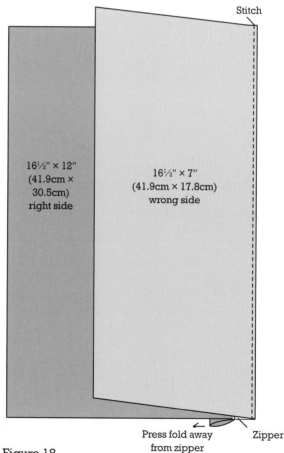

Figure 18

Bar Chart

Finished size: 60" × 80" (152.4cm × 203.2cm)

This project is the best of both worlds: the convenience of a precut and the satisfaction of using fabric from your stash. I had such fun digging through my stash for the greens in this quilt! I did have to add a couple of new ones, but most of them (including the 1 yard [0.9m] piece) were waiting for me in my fabric closet. While I don't consider myself a scrap quilter, this kind of monochromatic scrappiness is my favorite kind. Notice that the color range from green to yellow-green is fairly narrow while the value range is a bit broader.

Fabric Requirements & Supplies

Background: 1 jelly roll/roll up*

Contrast: (7) ¼ yard (0.2m) pieces**; (1) 1 yard (0.9m) piece

Batting: 66" × 86" (167.6cm × 218.4cm) (twin size)

Backing: 5 yards (4.6m)

Painter's tape (optional)

*A jelly roll is a collection of 2½" (6.4cm) strips

**Fat quarters not recommended

> **Fabric Note**
> The background fabric used in this project is Robert Kaufman Kona Cotton Solid in Riviera.

Cutting Instructions

Contrast

Cut (3) 2½" (6.4cm) × width of fabric (WOF) strips from each of the ¼ yard (0.2m) pieces.

Cut (11) 2½" (6.4cm) × WOF strips from the 1 yard (0.9m) piece. Set 8 aside for the binding. Trim the remaining 24 strips to 36½" (92.7cm) each.

Step 1: Sew the jelly roll strips together on the short ends. While the whole jelly roll will be needed, it might be easier to sew sets of 10 or 12 strips at a time.

Step 2: Cut the strips in Chart 1 from the long jelly roll strip. Mark the length of each piece as it is cut. (Painter's tape is handy for this; write the measurement on the roll before tearing it off.)

Step 3: Setting aside the 44½" (113cm) and 80½" (204.5cm) strips, pair the shortest piece with the longest piece in sets of 2 (Figure 1). Adding the length of these 2 strips together will give you a 45" (114.3cm) long piece. These sets will be sewn together with a contrast strip to make 1 of the columns in the quilt.

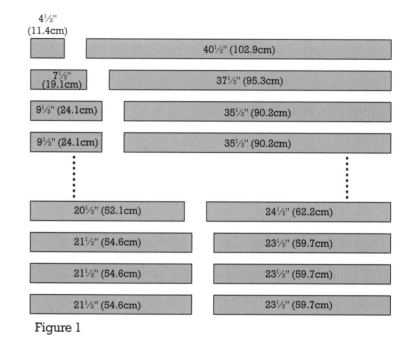

Figure 1

quantity	length	quantity	length	quantity	length
1	4½" (11.4cm)	1	19½" (49.5cm)	2	30½" (77.5cm)
1	7½" (19.1cm)	3	20½" (52.1cm)	1	31½" (80cm)
2	9½" (24.1cm)	3	21½" (54.6cm)	3	32½" (82.6cm)
3	12½" (31.8cm)	3	23½" (59.7cm)	2	35½" (90.2cm)
1	13½" (34.3cm)	3	24½" (62.2cm)	1	37½" (95.3cm)
2	14½" (36.8cm)	1	25½" (64.8cm)	1	40½" (102.9cm)
2	15½" (39.4cm)	2	26½" (67.3cm)		
2	17½" (44.5cm)	2	27½" (70cm)	1	44½" (113cm)
2	18½" (47cm)	2	29½" (74.9cm)	6	80½" (204.5cm)

Chart 1

Step 4: Lay out the background and contrast strips according to the layout table. Sew each column together on the short ends.

Sew the columns together first in pairs, then in pairs of 2 and so on until the quilt top is complete. *(Tip: When sewing long, straight seams, divide each strip into even quarters, mark with a pin and match these marks when sewing.)*

Top labels (left to right): 20½" (52.1cm), 35½" (90.2cm), 30½" (77.5cm), 40½" (102.9cm), 44½" (113cm), 35½" (90.2cm), 31½" (80cm), 20½" (52.1cm), 26½" (67.3cm), 23½" (59.7cm), 17½" (44.5cm), 12½" (31.8cm), 21½" (54.6cm), 32½" (82.6cm), 26½" (67.3cm), 21½" (54.6cm), 15½" (39.4cm), 12½" (31.8cm), 7½" (19.1cm), 24½" (62.2cm), 29½" (74.9cm), 19½" (49.5cm), 14½" (36.8cm), 17½" (44.5cm)

Middle labels: 80½" (204.5cm)

Bottom labels (left to right): 24½" (62.2cm), 9½" (24.1cm), 14½" (36.8cm), 4½" (11.4cm), 9½" (24.1cm), 13½" (34.3cm), 24½" (62.2cm), 18½" (47cm), 21½" (54.6cm), 27½" (70cm), 32½" (82.6cm), 23½" (59.7cm), 12½" (31.8cm), 18½" (47cm), 23½" (59.7cm), 29½" (74.9cm), 32½" (82.6cm), 37½" (95.3cm), 20½" (52.1cm), 15½" (39.4cm), 25½" (64.8cm), 30½" (77.5cm), 27½" (70cm)

Layout Table
Center contrast strips are 36½" (92.7cm)

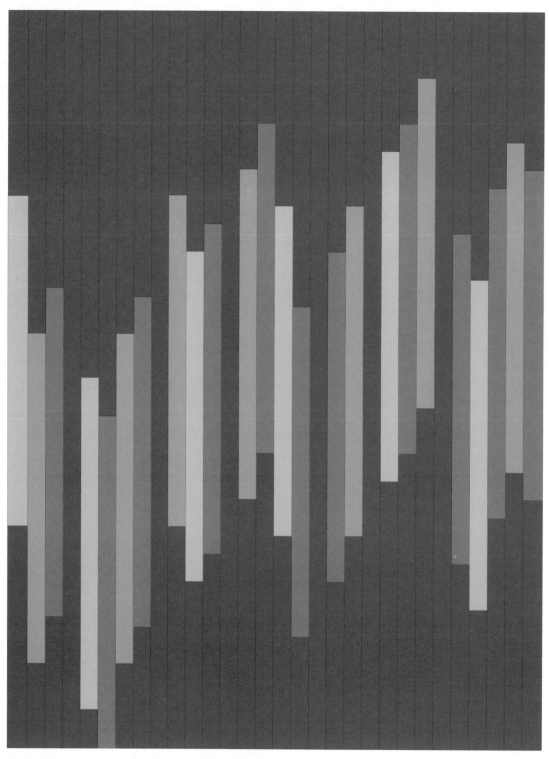

Step 5: Press the quilt top. Baste it together with the backing and batting. Quilt as desired. The quilt shown is quilted with straight lines in the ditch and down the center of each strip using blue thread in the blue sections and green thread in the green section.

Step 6: Bind the quilt with the contrast strips.

Figure 2

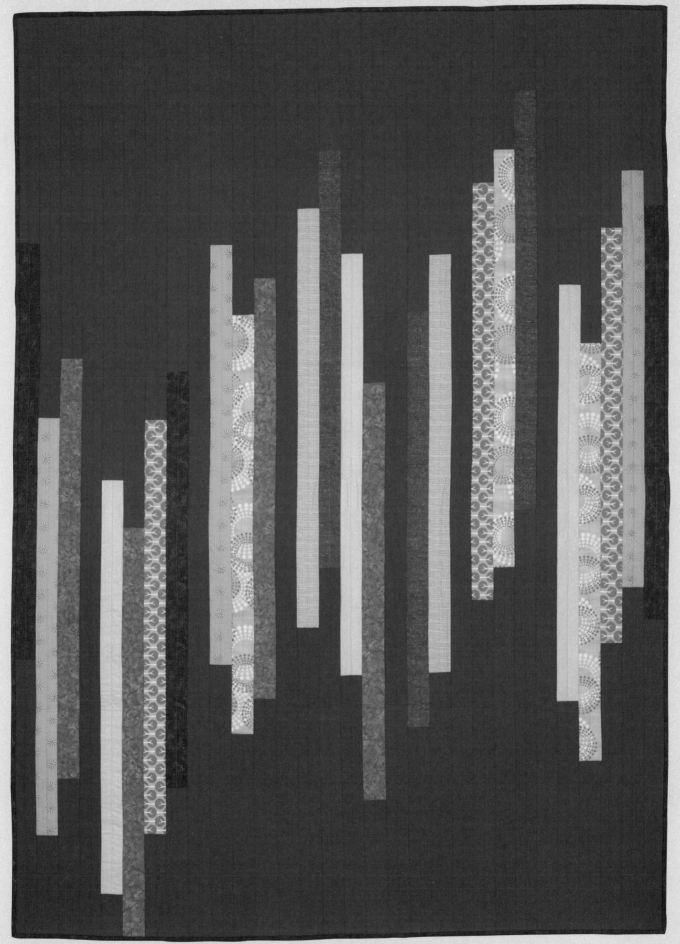

Fault Line

Finished size: 52" × 52" (132.1cm × 132.1cm)

I love this zigzag of bright white in the middle of the intense reds and oranges. To keep that intensity, both the color and value ranges of the oranges and reds are very narrow. A couple of the prints have a bit of white on them to add some variety, but their backgrounds are right in line with the rest of the fabrics.

Fabric Requirements & Supplies

Orange: (5) ⅜ yard (0.3m) pieces*

White: ⅜ yard (0.3m)

Red: (8) ¼ yard (0.2m) pieces* (for body of quilt); ¾ yard (0.7m) (for body and binding)

Batting: 58" × 58" (147.3cm × 147.3cm)

Backing: 3¼ yards (3m)

*Fat quarters not recommended

Fabric Note
Most of the reds and oranges in Fault Line came from my stash, with a few purchased to round things out. The white is Robert Kaufman Kona solid in White.

Cutting Instructions

Orange

Cut (3) 2½" (6.4cm) strips from each orange fabric. Mix them up so they are in a random order. Subcut as follows, marking each piece as it is cut:

Strip 1: 26" (66cm), 14" (35.6cm)

Strips 2–4: 24" (61cm), 16" (40.6cm)

Strips 5–8: 22" (55.9cm), 18" (45.7cm)

Strip 9: 22" (55.9cm), 14" (35.6cm)

Strip 10: (2) 20" (50.8cm)

Strip 11: 20" (50.8cm), 18" (45.7cm)

Strip 12: 18" (45.7cm), 12" (30.5cm)

Strip 13: 16" (40.6cm), 12" (30.5cm)

Note: There will be 2 extra strips.

White

Cut (4) 2½" (6.4cm) strips. Subcut (26) 2½" × 5" (6.4cm × 12.7cm) pieces.

Red

Cut (3) 2½" (6.4cm) strips from each ¼ yard (0.2m).

Cut (9) 2½" (6.4cm) strips from the ¾ yard (0.7m) piece. Set 6 of these strips aside for the binding.

Mix up the remaining strips and subcut as follows, again marking each piece as it is cut:

(2) 40½" (102.9cm) strips

(2) 38½" (97.8cm) strips

(4) 36½" (92.7cm) strips

(6) 34½" (87.6cm) strips

(3) 32½" (82.6cm) strips

(5) 30½" (77.5cm) strips

(3) 28½" (72.4cm) strips

(1) 26½" (67.3cm) strip

Note: There will be 1 extra strip.

Column	1	2	3	4	5	6	7	8	9	10	11	12	13
Orange	26" (66cm)	24" (61cm)	22" (55.9cm)	22" (55.9cm)	24" (61cm)	24" (61cm)	22" (55.9cm)	20" (50.8cm)	18" (45.7cm)	16" (40.6cm)	14" (35.6cm)	12" (30.5cm)	12" (30.5cm)
Red	26½" (67.3cm)	28½" (72.4cm)	30½" (77.5cm)	30½" (77.5cm)	28½" (72.4cm)	28½" (72.4cm)	30½" (77.5cm)	32½" (82.6cm)	34½" (87.6cm)	36½" (92.7cm)	38½" (97.8cm)	40½" (102.9cm)	40½" (102.9cm)

Column	14	15	16	17	18	19	20	21	22	23	24	25	26
Orange	14" (35.6cm)	16" (40.6cm)	18" (45.7cm)	18" (45.7cm)	16" (40.6cm)	16" (40.6cm)	18" (45.7cm)	20" (50.8cm)	22" (55.9cm)	22" (55.9cm)	20" (50.8cm)	18" (45.7cm)	18" (45.7cm)
Red	38½" (97.8cm)	36½" (92.7cm)	34½" (87.6cm)	34½" (87.6cm)	36½" (92.7cm)	36½" (92.7cm)	34½" (87.6cm)	32½" (82.6cm)	30½" (77.5cm)	30½" (77.5cm)	32½" (82.6cm)	34½" (87.6cm)	34½" (87.6cm)

Column Table

Step 1: Pair the orange and red strips together according to the Column Table, marking them with the appropriate column number.

Step 2: On the wrong side of a white rectangle, mark the center of the 5" (12.7cm) side on each side of the rectangle. Draw a line from the lower left corner to the center mark on the upper side of the rectangle. Draw a second line from the center mark on the lower side to the upper right corner of the rectangle (Figure 1). Make 15.

Step 3: Using the pairs of strips from the table that have a red or orange background (not gray), place the orange strip right side up on the table. Place the white rectangle right side down so that the lines are still going from lower left to upper right. Align the lower right corners of the fabrics. Pin in place.

Slide the red strip, right side up, under the other half of the white rectangle, aligning the upper left corners. Pin in place. Stitch along both drawn lines (Figure 2). Press the seams open and trim ¼" (6mm) away from the seams (Figure 3).

Step 4: For the remaining 11 white rectangles, mark the center on the wrong side of the 5" (12.7cm) side on each side of the rectangle. Draw a line from the upper left corner to the center mark on the lower side of the rectangle. Draw a second line from the center mark on the upper side to the lower right corner of the rectangle (Figure 4).

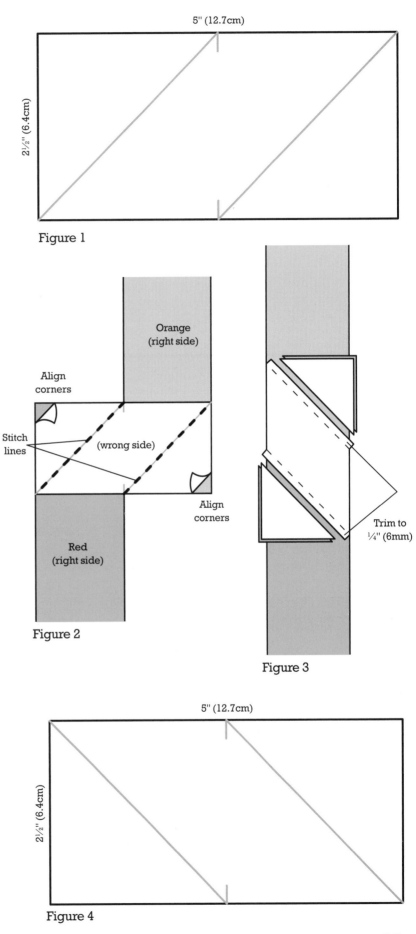

5" (12.7cm)

2½" (6.4cm)

Figure 1

Align corners

Orange (right side)

Stitch lines

(wrong side)

Align corners

Red (right side)

Figure 2

Trim to ¼" (6mm)

Figure 3

5" (12.7cm)

2½" (6.4cm)

Figure 4

Step 5: Using the pairs of strips from the table with the gray background, place the orange strip right side up on the table. Place the white rectangle right side down so that the lines are still going from upper left to lower right. Align the lower left corners of the fabrics. Pin in place.

Slide the red strip, right side up, under the other half of the white rectangle, aligning the upper right corners. Pin in place. Stitch along both drawn lines (Figure 5).

Press the seams open and trim ¼" (6mm) away from the seams (Figure 6).

Step 6: Lay out the columns in the same order as the Column Table. Sew the columns together first in pairs, then in pairs of 2 and so on until the quilt top is complete. Take care to match the white intersections.

Step 7: Press the quilt top. Baste together with the backing and batting. Quilt as desired. The project shown is quilted with large rectangles set at an angle and filled with quilting lines parallel to their edges. The idea was inspired by the plates of the earth that shift during an earthquake.

Step 8: Bind with the red strips (Figure 7).

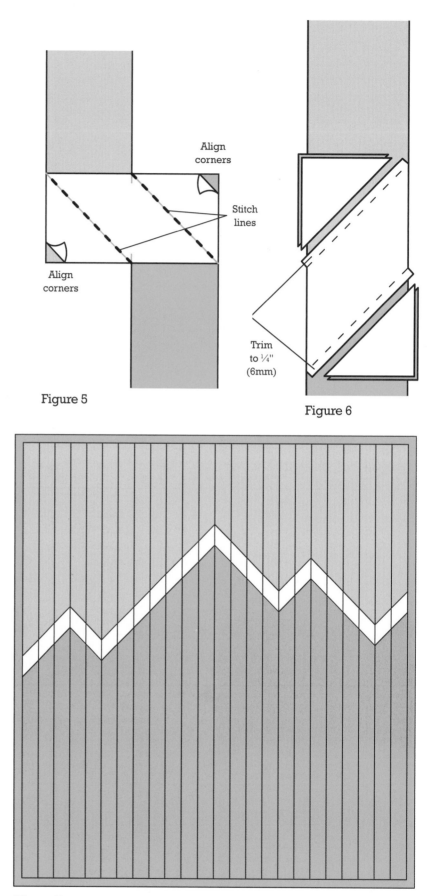

Figure 5

Figure 6

Figure 7

Epicenter

Finished size: 59" × 65½"
(149.9cm × 166.4cm)
Finished block: 6½" (16.5cm)

Epicenter started with the idea of cutting up a layer cake and making a quilt without adding any fabric. As I sketched my idea, I became focused on the shattered effect the seam lines created. Adding "leading" allowed me to make those lines a design feature. Limiting the color palette increased the focus on the graphic impact of the quilt. I can also see this being a great scrap project as long as the values are maintained.

Fabric Requirements & Supplies

Light: 2 fat quarters*

Medium: 6 fat quarters*

Dark: 7 fat quarters*

Leading and binding: 2 yards (1.8m)

Batting: 64" × 71" (162.6cm × 180.3cm)

Backing: 4 yards (3.7m)

*A fat quarter measures 18" × 22" (45.7cm × 55.9cm)

Fabric Note
The fabrics used in the project quilt are from a Robert Kaufman Kona Cotton True Blue Color Story fat quarter bundle.

Cutting Instructions

Light

From each fat quarter, cut (20) 3¼" (8.3cm) squares to total 40 squares.

Medium

From each fat quarter, cut (5) 3¼" (8.3cm) strips. Subcut (14) 3¼" × 6½" (8.3cm × 16.5cm) rectangles to total 80 rectangles.

Dark

From each fat quarter, cut (6) 6½" (16.5cm) squares to total 40 squares.

Leading/binding

Cut (48) 1" (2.5cm) strips. Set 4 aside for the leading borders on the left and bottom sides of the quilt. From the remaining strips, subcut (90) 7" (17.8cm) sections; (140) 6½" (16.5cm) sections; and (20) 3¼" (8.3cm) sections.

Cut (7) 2½" (6.4cm) strips for the binding.

NOTE: A blocks are from the light fabrics, B and C blocks are from the medium fabrics and D blocks are from the dark fabrics. Use the same fabric within each block.

Step 1: To make an A block: Sew a 3¼" (8.3cm) leading piece between 2 light 3¼" (8.3cm) squares; make 2. Sew a 6½" (16.5cm) leading piece between these 2 units. Sew a 6½" (16.5cm) leading piece to the right side of this unit and a 7" (17.8cm) leading piece to the top (Figure 1).

Make 10 blocks.

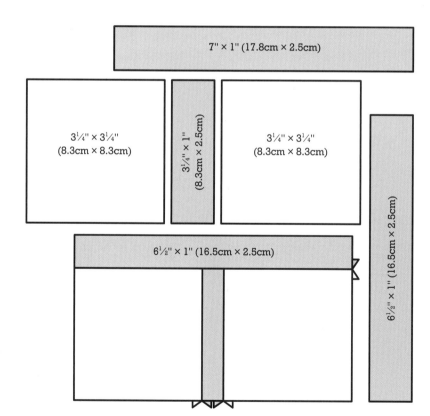

Figure 1
A block (light fabrics)

Step 2: To make a B block: Sew a 6½" (16.5cm) leading piece between 2 medium 3¼" × 6½" (8.3cm × 16.5cm) rectangles. With the leading section in a horizontal position, sew a 6½" (16.5cm) leading piece to the right side of this unit and a 7" (17.8cm) leading piece to the top (Figure 2).

Make 19 blocks.

Step 3: To make a C block: Sew a 6½" (8.3cm) leading piece between 2 medium 3¼" × 6½" (8.3cm × 16.5cm) rectangles. With the leading section in a vertical position, sew a 6½" (16.5cm) leading piece to the right side of this unit and a 7" (17.8cm) leading piece to the top (Figure 3).

Make 21 blocks.

Step 4: To make a D block: Sew a 6½" (16.5cm) leading piece to the right side of a dark 6½" (16.5cm) square and a 7" (17.8cm) leading piece to the top (Figure 4).

Make 40 blocks.

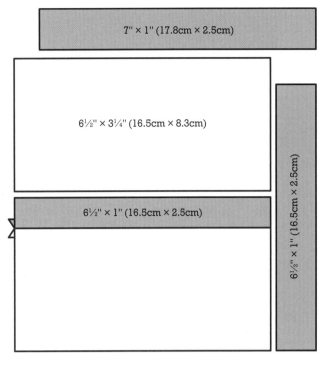

Figure 2
B block (medium fabrics)

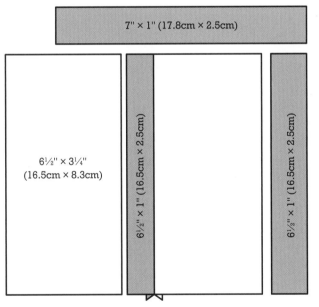

Figure 3
C block (medium fabrics)

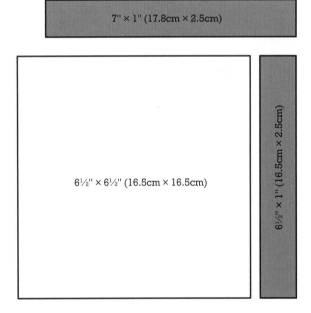

Figure 4
D block (dark fabrics)

Step 5: Lay out the blocks according to the Quilt Diagram. Sew the blocks into rows, and the rows into the quilt top.

Step 6: Sew four 1" (2.5cm) leading strips together on the short ends and cut 1 strip each 65½" (166.4cm) and 59½" (151.1cm). Sew the longer piece to the left side of the quilt top and the shorter piece to the bottom of the quilt top.

Step 7: Press the quilt top. Baste it together with the backing and batting. Quilt as desired. The project shown is quilted on the black leading and following the block design of the next lighter set of blocks.

Step 8: Bind the quilt with the 2½" (6.4cm) strips.

D	D	D	D	D	D	D	D	D
D	D	D	B	C	A	C	B	D
D	C	B	C	B	A	B	C	D
D	B	C	B	C	A	C	B	D
D	C	A	A	A	A	A	C	D
D	B	C	B	C	A	C	B	D
D	C	B	C	B	A	B	C	D
D	D	C	B	C	B	C	B	D
D	D	D	C	B	C	B	D	D
D	D	D	D	D	D	D	D	D

Quilt Diagram

Chapter 3

Squares and Rectangles

Squares and rectangles are the building blocks of many quilts. In this chapter, we take the outlines of squares and rectangles and focus on their impact. Daily Dining arranges rectangles and squares of various sizes into a pleasing geometric design for everyday place-mats. The rectangles in Bonsai were placed in a random fashion that became an abstract tree. By contrast, the impact of the squares on point in Classic comes from the repetition of each block and the orderly precision of the overall design.

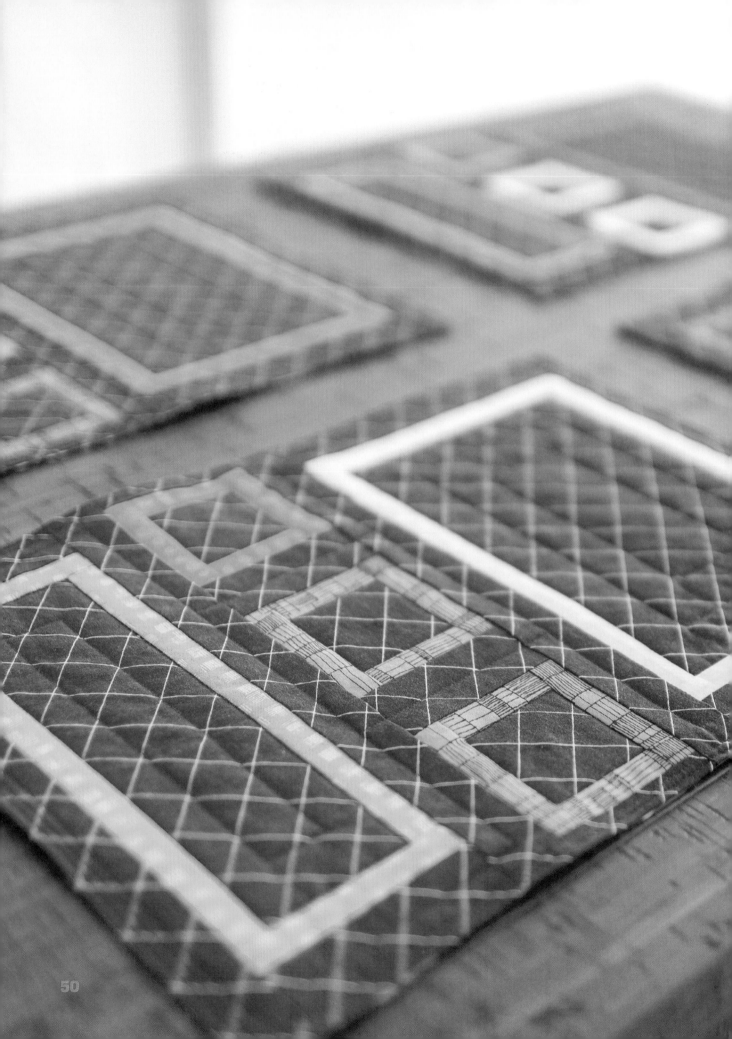

Daily Dining

Finished size: 12½" × 17½"
(31.8cm × 44.5cm) placemats

Add some quilty goodness to your everyday meals. It is hard to beat fun and function. Each of these four placemats has the accent fabrics in different positions so each family member can choose a different design. Go a step further and make napkins to match or "cheat" a bit like I do and purchase napkins and stitch around the edges with a different color for each family member.

Fabric Requirements & Supplies (all 4 placemats)

Accent fabrics: ⅛ yard (0.1m) or 1 fat eighth of 4 colors*

Background: 1 yard (0.9m)

Batting: (4) 12½ × 17½" (31.8cm × 44.5cm) pieces

Backing: 1 yard (0.9m)

*A fat eighth measures 9" × 22" (22.9cm × 55.9cm)

Fabric Note
The fabrics used in the placemats shown are from the Doe collection by Carolyn Friedlander for Robert Kaufman.

Cutting Instructions

Accent Colors

From each accent color, cut (3) 1" (2.5cm) strips from ⅛ yard (0.1m) or (7) 1" (2.5cm) from a fat eighth. Subcut (4) 9½" (24.1cm) strips; (2) 7½" (19.1cm) strips; (2) 4" (10.2cm) strips; (6) 3½" (8.9cm) strips; and (6) 2½" (6.4cm) strips.

Background

Cut (1) 6½" (16.5cm) strip. Subcut (4) 9½" (24.1cm) pieces (large rectangles).

Cut (1) 3" (7.6cm) strip. Subcut (4) 9½" (24.1cm) pieces (small rectangles).

Cut (1) 2½" (6.4cm) strip. Subcut (12) 2½" (6.4cm) squares.

Cut (4) 1¾" (4.4cm) strips. Subcut (8) 7½" (19.1cm) pieces, (8) 4" (10.2cm) pieces and (8) 3½" (8.9cm) pieces.

Cut (6) 1½" (3.8cm) strips. Subcut (16) 13" (33cm) pieces.

Cut (1) 1" (2.5cm) strip. Subcut (8) 3½" (8.9cm) pieces.

Backing

Cut (4) 13" × 18" (33cm × 45.7cm) pieces.

NOTE: Each of the accent fabrics is used to make each of the accent elements—that is one large rectangle, one small rectangle and three squares. Since all accent fabrics are 1" (2.5cm) wide strips, reference is made to their length only.

Step 1: Make 1 small rectangle using 1 of the accent fabrics as follows. Sew (2) 9½" (24.1cm) accent strips to either long side of the small background rectangle (3" × 9½" [7.6cm × 24.1cm]). Sew the 4" (10.2cm) accent strips to the top and bottom of the rectangle.

Sew a 1¾" × 4" (4.4cm × 10.2cm) background pieces to the top and bottom of the unit from above. Sew a 1½" × 13" (3.8cm × 33cm) background strip to each side of this piece (Figure 1).

Step 2: Make a large rectangle with the same accent color as Step 1. Sew two 9½" (24.1cm) accent strips to either long side of the large background rectangle (6½" × 9½" [16.5cm × 24.1cm]). Sew the 7½" (19.1cm) accent strips to the top and bottom of the rectangle.

Sew a 1¾" × 7½" (4.4cm × 19.1cm) background pieces to the top and bottom of the unit from above. Sew a 1½" × 13" (3.8cm × 33cm) background strip to each side of this piece (Figure 2).

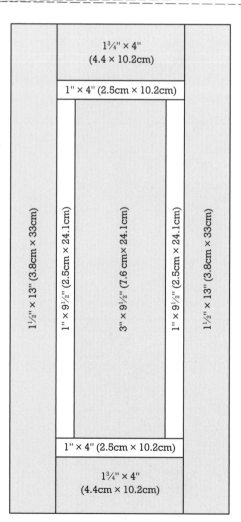

Figure 1
Small rectangle

Step 3: Make 3 squares with the same accent color as Step 1. Sew 2½" (6.4cm) accent strips on either side of a 2½" (6.4cm) background square. Sew 3½" (8.9cm) accent strips to the top and bottom of the square (Figure 3). Do not sew the remaining background pieces to the squares at this time.

Make a small rectangle, large rectangle and 3 squares from the other 3 accent colors.

Step 4: Layout the squares in 4 groups, following the square layout chart.

Sew a 1¾" × 3½" (4.4cm × 8.9cm) background piece to the top and bottom of the middle square of the group. Sew the top and bottom squares to this section. Sew a 1" × 3½" (2.5cm × 8.9cm) background piece to the top and bottom of the column of squares (Figure 4).

1	2	3	4
Gold	Gold	Orange	Orange
Gold	White	Green	White
Green	White	Green	Orange

Square Layout Chart

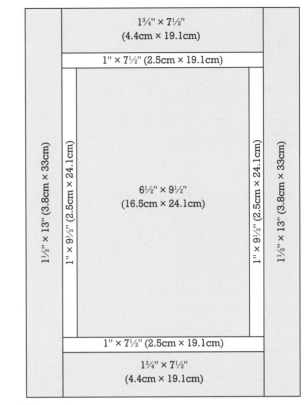

Figure 2
Large rectangle

1¾" × 7½" (4.4cm × 19.1cm)

1" × 7½" (2.5cm × 19.1cm)

1½" × 13" (3.8cm × 33cm)

1" × 9½" (2.5cm × 24.1cm)

6½" × 9½" (16.5cm × 24.1cm)

1" × 9½" (2.5cm × 24.1cm)

1½" × 13" (3.8cm × 33cm)

1" × 7½" (2.5cm × 19.1cm)

1¾" × 7½" (4.4cm × 19.1cm)

Figure 3
Squares

3½" (8.9cm)

2½" (6.4cm)

2½" (6.4cm) square

2½" (6.4cm)

3½" (8.9cm)

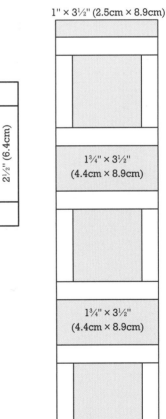

1" × 3½" (2.5cm × 8.9cm)

1¾" × 3½" (4.4cm × 8.9cm)

1¾" × 3½" (4.4cm × 8.9cm)

1" × 3½" (2.5cm × 8.9cm)

Figure 4

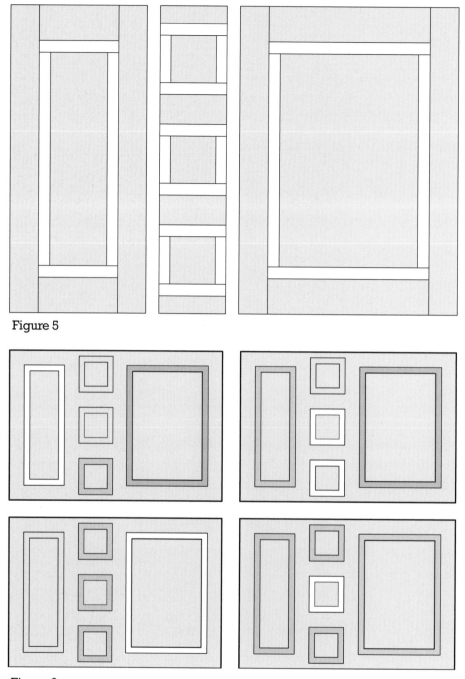

Figure 5

Figure 6

Step 5: Arrange the placemat sections as shown or as desired. Sew the 3 sections together to complete each placemat top (Figures 5 and 6).

Putting right sides together, place the backing with the placemat top, and pin. Beginning near the center of a

Step 6: To keep the clean lines of the design and to avoid bulk at the edges, the placemats are "pillowcased." Center the batting on the wrong side of the placemat top. Pin in place from the placemat top right side.

long side, stitch around all 4 sides with a ¼" (6mm) seam allowance, leaving a 5"–6" (12.7cm–15.2cm) opening for turning.

Step 7: Trim the corners and turn the placemats right side out. Press, folding the edges of the opening inside the placemat even with the edge. Stitch around the placemat ⅛" (3mm) and ¼" (6mm) from the edges.

Quilt the centers of the placemats as desired. The project shown is echo quilted and quilted in the ditch.

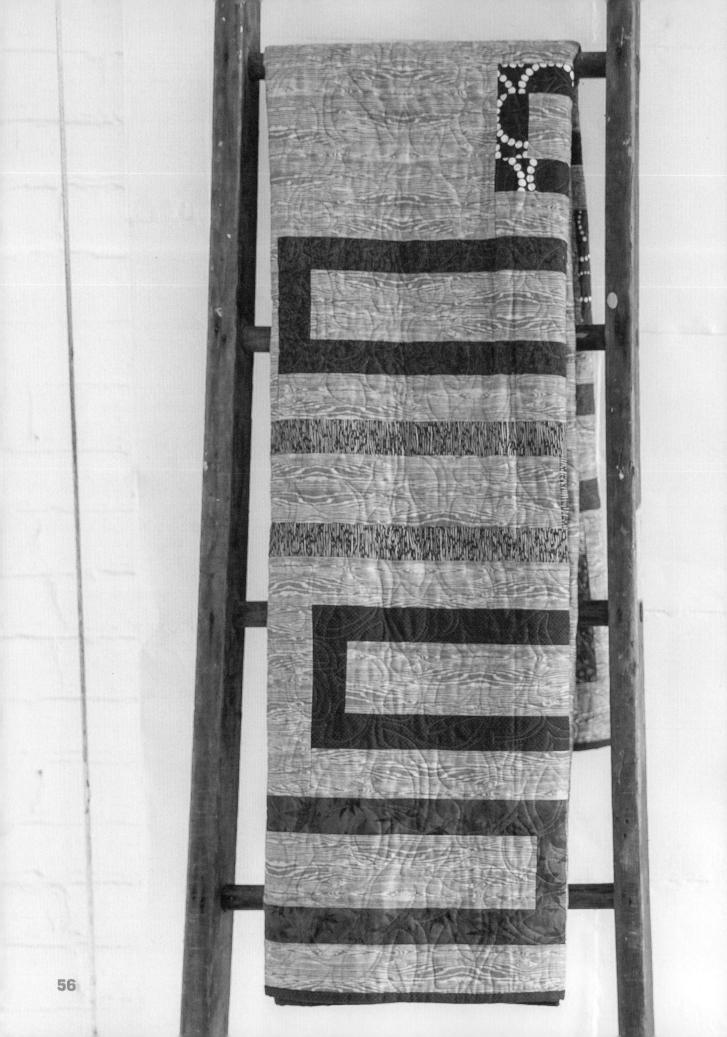

Bonsai

Finished size: 59" × 75" (149.9cm × 190.5cm)
Finished block: 6" × 19½" (15.2cm × 49.5cm)

Playing around with shapes is one of my favorite ways to design quilts. After experimenting with many different arrangements of these rectangles, I settled on this random design with one rectangle in each row. The overall design reminded me of a bonsai tree, so I added a second rectangle in the bottom row to give the trunk some stability. I see the brown rectangles as parts of the trunk peeking through the green leaves. A leafy fabric would be perfect for the green, but I couldn't resist the wood grain.

While I used just one fabric for the background, this project is perfect for using lots of pieces from your stash. Just be sure to stay in one color family (such as yellow-green) and to keep the value range fairly narrow. Too much variation will take the focus away from the shape formed by the brown sections. Finally, I added lots of free motion "leaves" to my tree during the quilting.

Fabric Requirements & Supplies

Blocks and binding (brown): 9 fat eighths* and ¾ yard (0.7m)

Background (green): 3¼ yards (3m)

Batting: 65" × 81" (165.1cm × 205.7cm)

Backing: 4⅔ yards (4.3m)

*A fat eighth measures 9" × 22" (22.9cm × 55.9cm)

> **Fabric Note**
> *The background fabric used in this project is Wood Grain from True Colors by Joel Dewberry for Free Spirit. The browns are from my stash.*

Cutting Instructions

Brown

Cut (2) 2" × 20" (5.1cm × 50.8cm) and (2) 2" × 3½" (5.1cm × 8.9cm) strips from each fabric.

Cut (7) 2½" (6.4cm) strips from the rest of the ¾ yard (0.7m) piece for the binding.

Green

Cut (8) 8½" (21.6cm) strips for rows. Subcut following Table 1.

Cut (6) 2½" (6.4cm) strips for sashing. Set 2 strips aside for the border and subcut the rest into 20" (50.8cm) pieces.

Cut (1) 6½" (16.5cm) strip for the bottom row. Subcut (1) 13" (33cm), (1) 5" (12.7cm) and (1) 3½" (8.9cm) piece. Label the pieces as "9L," "9C" and "9R" respectively.

Cut (7) 3½" (8.9cm) strips for the centers and top border. Set 2 strips aside for the border and subcut the rest into (10) 17" (43.2cm) pieces.

NOTE: Use one brown fabric for each block and always press to the background.

Step 1: Sew the 2" × 3½" (5.1cm × 8.9cm) brown strips to each side of a 3½" × 17" (8.9cm × 43.2cm) background piece. Sew the 2" × 20" (5.1cm × 50.8cm) brown pieces to the top and bottom of this unit (Figure 1). Make 10 blocks.

Step 2: Sew a 2½" × 20" (6.4cm × 50.8cm) sashing piece to the bottom of 8 blocks (Figure 2).

Step 3: To add the background to rows 1–8, sew a block in between a matching set of background pieces from Table 1, keeping the L on the left side of the block, the R on the right side and the sashing on the bottom (Figure 3).

Step 4: To make the bottom row, sew the remaining 2 blocks in between the background pieces as follows: 9L; block; 9C; block; 9R (Figure 4).

Sew the rows together in number order.

Step 5: Make the borders: Sew the short ends of the 3½" (8.9cm) background strips together and trim to 59½" (151.1cm). Sew to the top of the quilt.

Sew the short ends of the 2½" (6.4cm) background strips together and trim to 59½" (151.1cm). Sew to the bottom of the quilt (Figure 5).

Step 6: Press the quilt top. Baste together with the backing and batting. Quilt as desired. The sample project is quilted in an allover abstract leaf pattern.

Step 7: Bind the quilt with the brown strips.

Row	Left	Right
1	34" (86.4cm)	6½" (16.5cm)
2	22" (55.9cm)	18½" (47cm)
3	14" (35.6cm)	26½" (67.3cm)
4	22" (55.9cm)	18½" (47cm)
5	29" (73.7cm)	11½" (29.2cm)
6	19" (48.3cm)	21½" (54.6cm)
7	14" (35.6cm)	26½" (67.3cm)
8	21" (53.3cm)	19½" (49.5cm)

Table 1
The pieces cut for the left side of the quilt are in whole inches and the ones for the right side of the quilt are half inches—each set should add up to 40½" (102.9cm). Label the pieces with the row number and L or R.

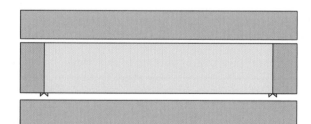

Figure 1

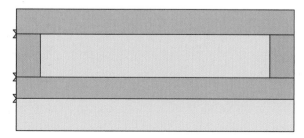

Figure 2

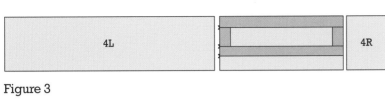

Figure 3

Figure 4

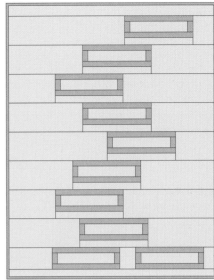

Figure 5

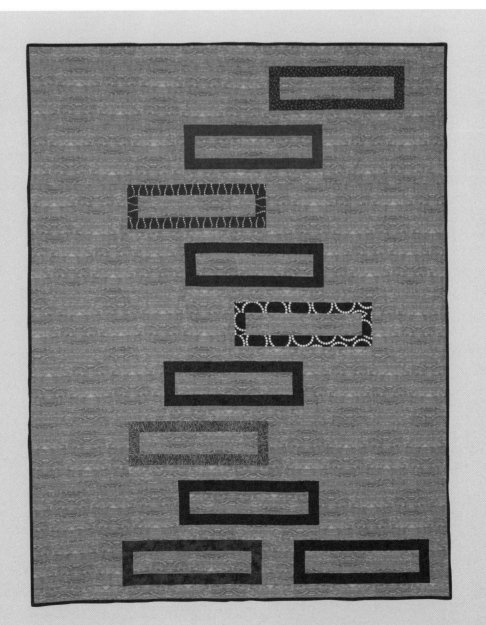

Classic

Finished size: 75" × 75" (190.5cm × 190.5cm)
Finished block: 9" (22.9cm)

There are so many beautiful, classic things about this quilt, yet it has such a new feel. You can't get much more classic in quilting than a log cabin variation. Reducing the number of colors and using solids removes the focus from the piecing and places it on the overall design. The classic layout somehow reminded me of little girls taking ballet in their black leotards and pink tights. Pink isn't a classic color for a quilt, but I love how it plays with the black—it's feminine sophistication at its best.

Fabric Requirements & Supplies

Background (pink): 5 yards (4.6m)

Accent (black): 1¾ yards (1.6m)

Batting: 81" × 81" (205.7cm × 205.7cm)

Backing: 4¾ yards (4.3m)

Fabric Note
The fabrics used in this project are
Robert Kaufman Kona cotton solids
in Baby Pink and Black.

Cutting Instructions

All strips are cut to the width of the fabric.

Pink

Cut (2) 14" (35.6cm) strips for the setting triangles. Subcut these into (4) 14" (35.6cm) squares and (2) 7¼" (18.4cm) squares. Cut the 14" (35.6cm) squares in half diagonally twice (like an X) (Figure 1). Cut the 7¼" (18.4cm) squares in half diagonally once.

Cut (8) 5½" (14cm) strips for the borders.

For the blocks, cut (4) 5" (12.7cm) strips. Subcut (25) 5" (12.7cm) squares.

Cut (11) 3½" (8.9cm) strips. Subcut (32) 9½" (24.1cm) pieces and (32) 3½" (8.9cm) squares.

Cut (22) 2" (5.1cm) strips. Subcut (50) 9½" (24.1cm) pieces, (50) 6½" (16.5cm) pieces and (16) 2" (5.1cm) squares.

Black

Cut (8) 2½" (6.4cm) strips for the binding.

Cut (27) 1¼" (3.2cm) strips for the blocks. Subcut these into (50) 6½" (16.5cm) pieces, (50) 5" (12.7cm) pieces, (32) 3½" (8.9cm) pieces and (32) 2" (5.1cm) pieces. Set the remaining 7 strips aside for the border.

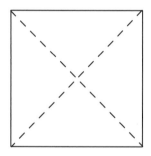

Figure 1

NOTE: Since all black strips are 1¼" (3.2cm) wide, reference will be made to the length only. Press to the black.

Step 1: Make Block A: Sew a black 5" (12.7cm) strip to the sides of a pink 5" (12.7cm) square. Sew a black 6½" (16.5cm) strip to the top and bottom of the square.

Sew a pink 2" × 6½" (5.1cm × 16.5cm) piece to the sides of the unit from above. Sew a pink 2" × 9½" (5.1cm × 24.1cm) strip to the top and bottom of the same unit (Figure 2). Make 25.

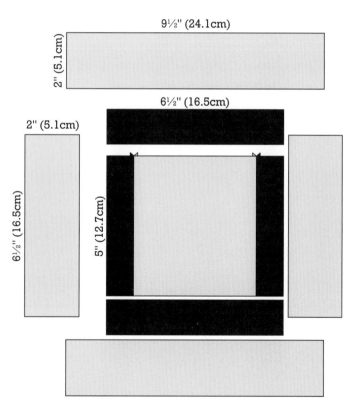

Figure 2: Block A
Make 25

Step 2: Make Block B: Sew a black 2" (5.1cm) strip to the sides of a pink 2" (5.1cm) square. Sew a black 3½" (8.9cm) strip to the top and bottom of the square.

Sew a pink 3½" (8.9cm) square to the sides of the unit from above. Sew a pink 3½" × 9½" (8.9cm × 24.1cm) strip to the top and bottom of the same unit (Figure 3). Make 16.

Step 3: Sew the blocks together in rows alternating the A and B blocks as follows (Figure 4):

ABA (2 rows)
ABABA (2 rows)
ABABABA (2 rows)
ABABABABA (1 rows)
There should be 2 A blocks remaining.

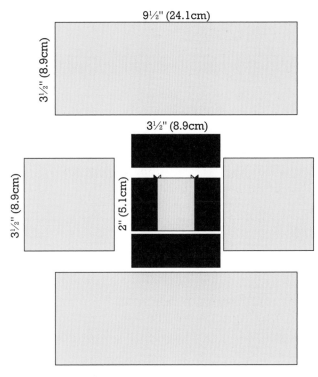

Figure 3: Block B
Make 16

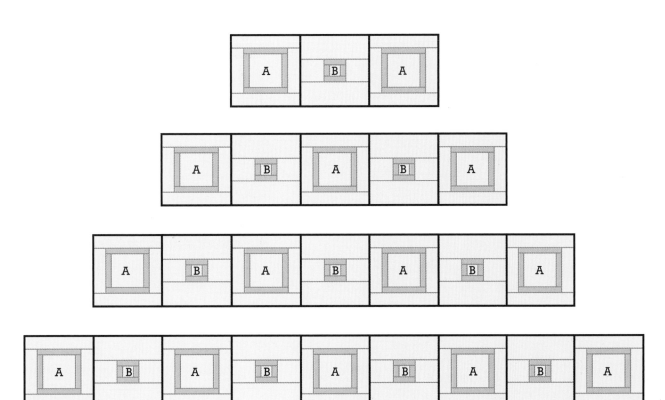

Figure 4

Step 4: Sew the short side of 1 of the setting triangles from the 14" (35.6cm) squares to the sides of the 2 single A blocks and to the end of each row, except the longest row (Figure 5).

Step 5: Sew the long side of the setting triangles from the 7¼" (18.4cm) squares to the top of the single A blocks and to the ends of the longest row (Figure 6).

Step 6: Sew the rows together in an on-point setting as shown (Figure 7).

Step 7: Sew the 7 black 1¼" (3.2cm) strips together on the short ends and trim 2 to 64¼" (163.2cm) and 2 to 65¾" (167cm). Sew the shorter pieces to the sides of the quilt and the longer pieces to the top and bottom.

Step 8: Sew the pink 5½" (14cm) border strips together on the short ends and trim 2 to 65¾" (167cm) and 2 to 75¾" (192.4cm). Sew the shorter pieces to the sides of the quilt and the longer pieces to the top and bottom.

Step 9: Press the quilt top. Baste together with the backing and batting. Quilt as desired. Classic was quilted with straight diagonal lines echoing the piecing.

Step 10: Bind with the black strips.

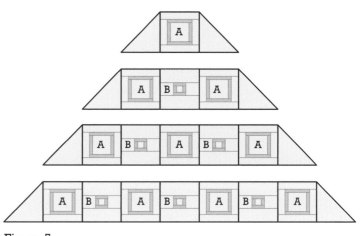

Figure 5

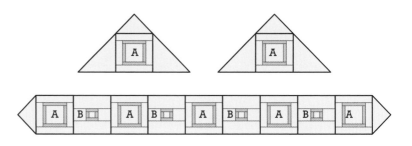

Figure 6

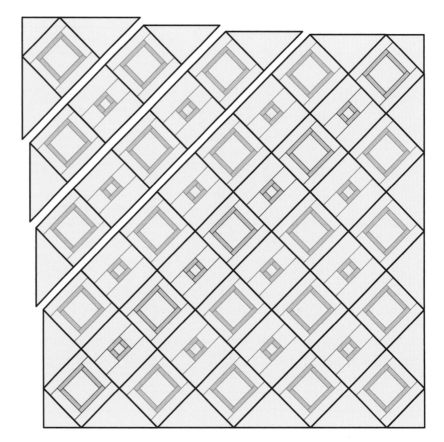

Figure 7

Chapter 4

Diamonds and Hexagons

Diamonds and hexagons are such fun shapes. Deciding whether to piece or appliqué these quilts took some thought. When working with lines that are not simple angles, the piecing can be difficult to structure for easy repetition (that kind of geometry is not my strong suit!). Park Estate seemed a natural for piecing, but Molecule and Facets were a better fit for appliqué. I love the directness of appliqué—you can design exactly the shape you want and put it exactly where you want. The rhythm of the process of stitching over the raw edges of the appliqué is one of my favorite parts of quilting.

Molecule

Finished size: 24" × 32" (61cm × 81.2cm)
Finished block: approx. 7" × 8" (17.8cm × 20.3cm)

This quilt began several years ago when English Paper Piecing (EPP) was the latest technique to try. As someone who loves handwork, it seemed a natural fit for me. However, somehow, I didn't enjoy the process of EPP the same way I do hand appliqué or even hand stitching a binding. So I drew what I called "My Hexy Quilt": big hexies with open centers in one little group and lots of negative space. Looking back at it later, I called it "Molecule" after the (vague) memory of drawings done in high school chemistry (and in honor of my father, a retired professor of chemistry).

Now the little group of hexies makes me think of a family—fitting perfectly with the baby size of this little quilt. I love how what you see can change over time. What do you see in this group of shapes?

Fabric Requirements & Supplies

Background: ¾ yard (0.7m) gray

Hexies: 9" (22.9cm) square of 5 prints (plum, teal, olive, orange, gold)

Binding: ⅓ yard (0.3m)

Batting: 30" × 42" (76.2cm × 106.7cm)

Backing: 1 yard (0.9m)

Fusible web: 1 yard (0.9m)

Stabilizer (optional): 1 yard (0.9m)

Thread to match hexy fabrics

Hexagon template (see Templates)

Fabric Note
The background fabric used in this project is Robert Kaufman Kona Cotton Solids in Coal..

Cutting Instructions

Background

Cut a 24½" (62.2cm) strip and trim to 32½" (82.6cm)

Binding

Cut (3) 2½" (6.4cm) strips

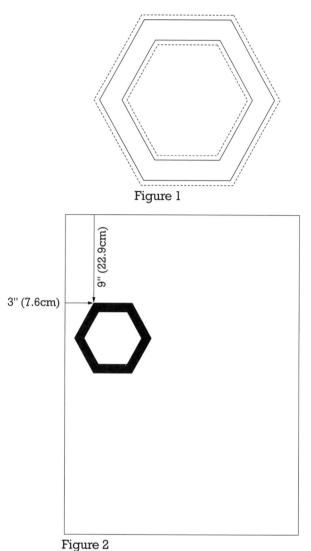

Figure 1

3" (7.6cm)

9" (22.9cm)

Figure 2

Step 1: Trace the hexagon pattern onto the paper side of the fusible web 5 times, leaving at least ½" (1.3cm) between the shapes.

Cut out the shapes approximately ¼" (6mm) outside the traced lines, including the centers (Figure 1).

Fuse 1 hexy shape to the wrong side of each hexy fabric. Cut along the traced lines. Remove the paper backing.

Step 2: Position the top left corner of the first hexy 9" (22.9cm) down from the top raw edge of the background and 3" (7.6cm) from the left raw edge (Figure 2).

Place the remaining hexies as shown (Figure 3), leaving approximately ¼" (6mm) between them. Don't measure; just make sure the spaces look fairly even. Note that the hexies are positioned so that the top and bottom are flat, not rotated so they are on point.

Step 3: Fuse in place. Stitch along the raw edges using a slightly open zigzag and matching thread.

Step 4: Press the quilt top. Baste together with the backing and batting. Quilt as desired. Molecule is echo quilted with hexagons the same size as the appliqué.

Step 5: Bind with the 2½" (6.4cm) strips.

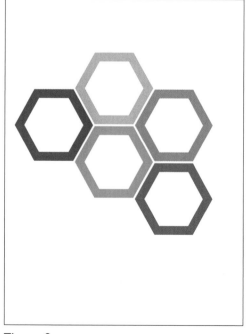

Figure 3

Facets

Finished size: 60" × 60" (152.4cm × 152.4cm)

Rugs are some of my favorite inspiration sources! A few years ago I saw a picture of a rug that was simple zigzag lines set in opposing directions to form the suggestion of diamonds where the lines didn't quite meet. The idea of doing something with large diamonds has stayed in my mind ever since. Facets gave me the opportunity to play with that idea. I enjoy the symmetry of the sets of four diamonds mixed with the asymmetry of the layout.

Fabric Requirements & Supplies

Background (blue): 3¼ yards (3m)

Contrast (white): 1½ yards (1.4m)

Batting: 66" × 66" (167.6cm × 167.6cm)

Backing: 3¾ yards (3.4m)

Fusible webbing: 3¼ yards (3m)

Stabilizer (optional): 3¼ yards (3m)

Diamond template (see Templates)

Fabric Note
The fabrics used in this project are Robert Kaufman Kona Cotton Solids in Stratosphere and White.

Cutting Instructions

Background

Cut and label the following pieces A–I:

Cut (2) 20" (50.8cm) (A) strips, (1) 17" (43.2cm) (F) strip and (1) 5" (12.7cm) (C) strip. Subcut all of these strips to 40" (101.6cm).

Cut (1) 2" (5.1cm) strip. Subcut to 36½" (92.7cm) (G).

Cut (1) 24½" (62.2cm) strip. Subcut (1) 19½"(49.5cm) (D) piece and (1) 2" (5.1cm) (E) piece.

Cut (1) 19½" (49.5cm). Subcut to (1) 19½" (49.5cm) (H) square and (2) 9" (22.9cm) (B and I) pieces.

Contrast

Cut (7) 2½" (6.4cm) strips for the binding.

Step 1: Trace the diamond pattern twice and tape together on the dotted line to create the diamond template (Figure 1).

Trace 9 diamonds approximately ½" (1.3cm) apart onto the paper side of the fusible web. Cut the diamonds apart leaving about ¼" (6mm) around the traced lines.

Step 2: Following the manufacturer's directions, fuse the diamonds to the wrong side of the contrast fabric. Cut out on the outer and inner traced lines. (Figure 2).

Step 3: Fold an A background block in half vertically and horizontally, and lightly press the fold lines. Place 4 diamonds ½" (1.3cm) from the raw edges, lining up the points of the diamond closest to the raw edge with the fold lines of the block. Fuse in place and stitch around all raw edges using a zigzag stitch, using the stabilizer if desired. Repeat once more for 2 A blocks.

Step 4: For the B block, fold the background block in half vertically only, and lightly press the fold lines. Place one diamond ½" (1.3cm) below the top raw edge, centering it along the fold line (Figure 4).

Note that this diamond is NOT centered vertically. There should be about 2" (5.1cm) from the bottom point of the diamond to the bottom raw edge of the background. Fuse the diamond in place and stitch around all raw edges using a zigzag stitch, using the stabilizer if desired.

Step 5: Sew piece C to the left side of an A block. Sew piece D to the top and piece E to the bottom to form Unit 1 (Figure 5).

Step 6: Sew piece F to the right side of the other A block. Sew piece G to the top to form Unit 2 (Figure 6).

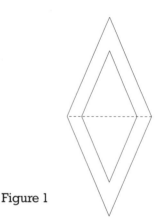

Figure 1

Wrong side

Figure 2

20" (50.8cm)

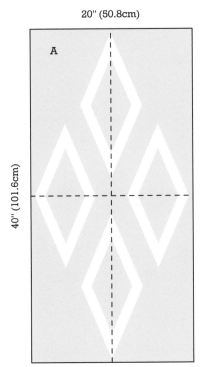

A

40" (101.6cm)

Figure 3

9" (22.9cm)

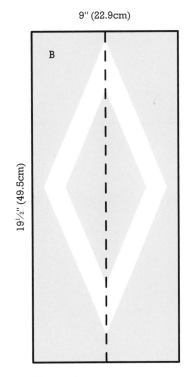

B

19½" (49.5cm)

Figure 4

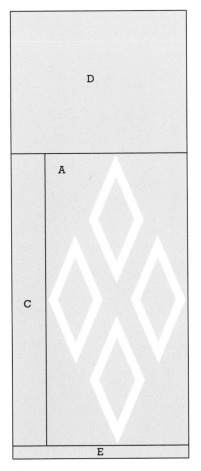

D

A

C

E

Figure 5
Unit 1

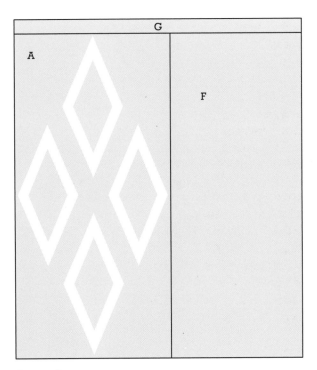

G

A

F

Figure 6
Unit 2

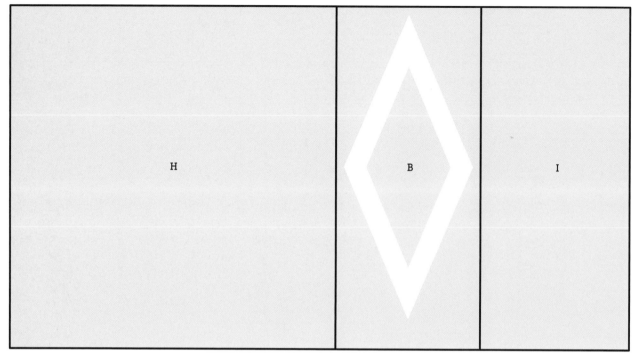

Figure 7
Unit 3

Step 7: Sew piece H to the left side of the B block (the diamond should be at the upper edge) and I to the right side to form Unit 3 (Figure 7).

Step 8: Sew Unit 3 to the bottom of Unit 2. Sew this unit to the right side of Unit 1 to complete the quilt top (Figure 8).

Step 9: Press the quilt top. Baste the top together with the backing and batting. Quilt as desired. Facets is quilted in a diamond grid that echoes the angles of the diamonds on the quilt.

Step 10: Bind with the 2½" (6.4cm) contrast strips.

Figure 8

Park Estate

Finished size: 86" × 86" (218.4cm × 218.4cm)
Finished size: 22" (55.9cm)

Park Estate was inspired by some pretty brickwork on one of the buildings in the city where I live. When I'd finished distilling it down to lines, it reminded me of a wrought iron gate on a park or estate. I was tempted to make the background color a rich red or deep eggplant, but this is a bed-size quilt and that much of one intense color can be overwhelming. I'm a huge fan of neutrals and their gentle and calming feel, and this quilt was a good one to use a quieter color scheme.

Fabric Requirements & Supplies

Background (dark): 5¾ yards (5.3m)

Contrast (light): 3 yards (2.7m)*

Batting: 92" × 92" (233.7cm × 233.7cm)

Backing: 6¼ yards (5.7m)

*You'll need 41 usable inches (104.1cm) of contrast fabric. If not, purchase an extra ½ yard (0.5m)

Fabric Note
The fabrics used in this project are Robert Kaufman Kona Cotton Solids in Stone and White.

Cutting Instructions

Background

Cut (4) 4½" (11.4cm) strips. Subcut (36) 4½" (11.4cm) squares.

Cut (4) 3" (7.6cm) strips.

Cut (1) 7¼" (18.4cm) strip.

Cut (6) 11" (27.9cm) strips for the setting triangles. Subcut (18) 11" (27.9cm) squares and cut these in half diagonally.

Cut (8) 2½" (6.4cm) strips for sashing. Set 2 aside. Subcut (1) 22½" (57.2cm) piece from each remaining strip.

Cut (8) 3½" (8.9cm) strips for the inner border.

Cut (9) 4½" (11.4cm) strips for the outer border.

Contrast

Cut (50) 1½" (3.8cm) strips for the blocks and border. From these, set aside 11 strips for the connector units and middle border. From each of the next 18 strips, cut (1) 22½" (57.2cm) piece, (2) 6½" (16.5cm) pieces, and (1) 4½" (11.4cm) piece. From the next 6 strips, cut (36) 6½" (16.5cm) pieces. From the next 6 strips, cut (54) 4½" (11.4cm) pieces. From the remaining 9 strips, cut (18) 20½" (52.1cm) pieces.

Cut (9) 2½" (6.4cm) strips for the binding.

Step 1: To make the square units, sew 4½" (11.4cm) contrast pieces to opposite sides of a 4½" (11.4cm) background square. Sew 6½" (16.5cm) pieces to the remaining sides of the background square. (Note: When framing squares like this, I always sew the sides first and the top and bottom second.) Make 36 (Figure 1).

Step 2: Make the short connector A units. Use 3 of the 11 contrast strips set aside. Sew a width-of-fabric (WOF) contrast strip between 2 WOF 3" (7.6cm) background strips. Subcut (18) 2¼" (5.7cm) Connector A pieces (Figure 2).

Step 3: Make the long connector B units. Sew WOF strips together in the following order: 3" (7.6cm) background; 1½" (3.8cm) contrast; 7¼" (18.4cm) background; 1½" (3.8cm) contrast; 3" (7.6cm) background. Subcut (9) 2¼" (5.7cm) Connector B pieces (Figure 3).

Step 4: To complete a block, sew a Connector A unit in between 2 square units (Figure 4). Make 2.

Sew a Connector B unit in between the 2 units from above (Figure 5)

Sew a setting triangle to each side of the above unit. Note: Begin with 2 opposite sides first (Figure 6). Trim the block to 20½" (52.1cm) square if needed. The diamond points should be about ½" (1.3cm) from the raw edge of the fabric. The center part of the block is meant to float a bit apart from the next round of strips.

Sew 20½" (52.1cm) contrast pieces to opposite sides of the block. Sew 22½" (57.2cm) contrast pieces to the remaining sides of the block (Figure 7). Make 9 blocks.

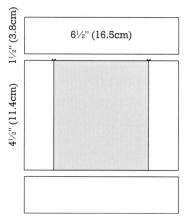

Figure 1: Square Unit

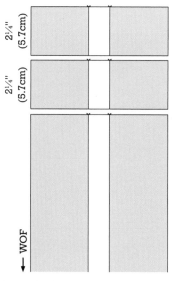

Figure 2: Connector A Units

2¼" (5.7cm)

2¼" (5.7cm)

← WOF

Figure 3: Connector B Units

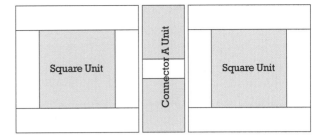

Square Unit | Connector A Unit | Square Unit

Figure 4

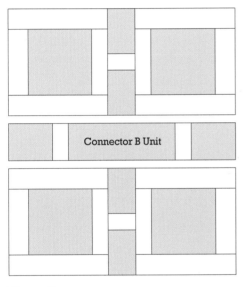

Connector B Unit

Figure 5

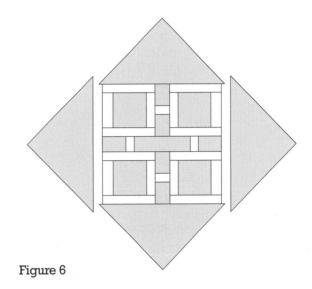

Figure 6

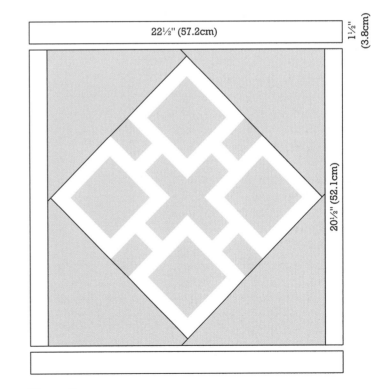

22½" (57.2cm)

1½" (3.8cm)

20½" (52.1cm)

Figure 7

Step 5: Lay the quilt blocks out in 3 rows of 3. Sew the 22½" (57.2cm) sashing pieces in between the blocks of each row.

Sew a leftover sashing piece (from subcutting) to each end of the remaining 2 WOF sashing strips, and subcut each one to 70½" (179.1cm). Sew these between the rows of blocks (Figure 8).

Step 6: For the inner border, sew the 3½" (8.9cm) background strips together on the short ends and subcut 2 to 70½"(179.1cm) and 2 to 76½" (194.3cm). Sew the shorter strips to the sides of the quilt center and the longer strips to the top and bottom.

For the middle border, sew the 8 remaining 1½" (3.8cm) contrast strips together on the short ends and subcut 2 to 76½" (194.3cm) and 2 to 78½" (199.4cm). Sew the shorter strips to the sides of the quilt center and the longer strips to the top and bottom.

For the outer border, sew the 4½" (11.4cm) background strips together on the short ends and subcut 2 to 78½" (199.4cm) and 2 to 86½" (219.7cm). Sew the shorter strips to the sides of the quilt center and the longer strips to the top and bottom (Figure 9).

Step 7: Press the quilt top. Baste the top together with the backing and batting. Quilt as desired. Park Estate is quilted in an argyle-inspired design.

Step 8: Bind with the 2½" (6.4cm) contrast strips.

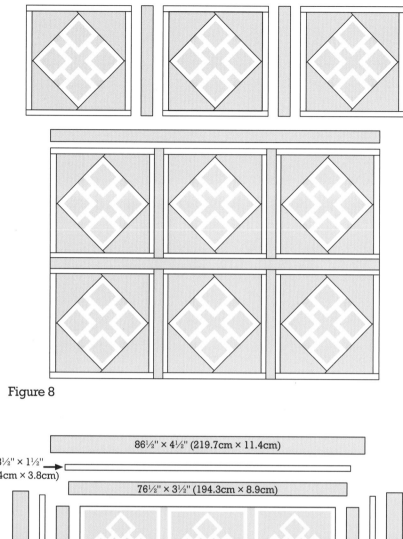

Figure 8

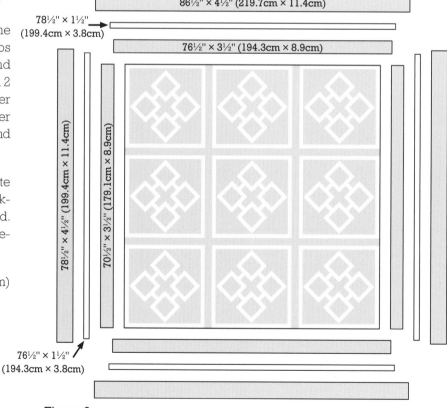

86½" × 4½" (219.7cm × 11.4cm)

78½" × 1½" (199.4cm × 3.8cm)

76½" × 3½" (194.3cm × 8.9cm)

78½" × 4½" (199.4cm × 11.4cm)

70½" × 3½" (179.1cm × 8.9cm)

76½" × 1½" (194.3cm × 3.8cm)

Figure 9

Chapter 5

Circles and Curves

A circle is so perfectly complete while a curve feels inviting—like a bend in a path you want to follow. The grid of bold circles in Road Work feels solid, while the random arrangement in Watermark has a more organic flow, and the curves of Forever leave the circles almost to your imagination.

Watermark

Finished size: 13½" × 30" (34.3cm × 76.2cm)

They say inspiration is everywhere and it is true! Watermark was inspired by a towel rack in a bedroom I saw on Pinterest. After sketching the design, the circles reminded me of the marks a water glass leaves on a wooden table. The orange print rectangles and binding add a bit of color to an otherwise neutral color scheme.

Fabric Requirements & Supplies

Background: ½ yard (0.5m)

Accent (orange print): (2) 4½" × 12½" (11.4cm × 31.8cm) pieces

Contrast (white circles): 1 fat quarter (not a long skinny one)

Binding (orange print): ¼ yard (0.2m)

Batting: 20" × 36" (50.8cm × 91.4cm)

Backing: 20" × 36" (50.8cm × 91.4cm)

½ yard (0.5m) freezer paper

Circle template pattern (see Templates)

Removable marking pencil

Fabric Note

The fabrics used in this project are from the Reel Time line by Zen Chic for Moda.

Cutting Instructions

Background

Cut a 14" × 30½" (35.6cm × 77.5cm) piece.

Accent

Cut the vertical accent piece 3½" × 12" (8.9cm × 30.5cm) (A).

Cut the horizontal accent piece 4" × 10½" (10.2cm × 26.7cm) (B).

Contrast

Cut (7) ¾" (1.9cm) wide bias strips, trim to 17" (43.2cm).

Binding

Cut (3) 2½" (6.4cm) strips.

Step 1: Press under ¼" (6mm) on all sides of accent piece A. Press under ¼" (6mm) on both long sides and the right short side of accent piece B.

Step 2: Position piece A 1¾" (4.4cm) from the top raw edge of the background fabric and 2½" (6.4cm) from the right raw edge. Straight stitch along the folded edges.

Position piece B 19¼" (48.9cm) from the top raw edge and align the left raw edges. Straight stitch along the folded edges (Figure 1).

Step 3: Using Table 1 and the removable marking pencil, make dots on the background fabric at the coordinates listed for each circle. These dots mark the center of each "watermark" circle.

Step 4: Trace the circle pattern 7 times onto the freezer paper. Cut out along the line. Fold the circles into 4 to mark the centers. Cut a small X at the center of each circle along the folds, and fold back a corner to allow the marks on the background fabric to be seen.

Match the marked dots on the background with the centers of the circles, and press the freezer paper circles in place using a dry iron. There should be small gaps between them as the bias will cover the lines and not all finished circles touch other circles. Using the removable marking pencil, trace around each circle (Figure 2).

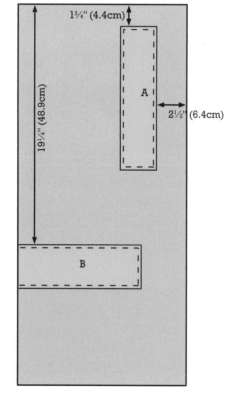

Figure 1

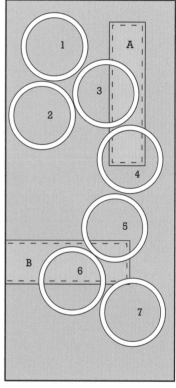

Figure 2

Circle number	Placement from left raw edge	Placement from top raw edge
1	4" (10.2cm)	3¾" (9.5cm)
2	3" (7.6cm)	9¼" (23.5cm)
3	8¼" (21cm)	7½" (19.1cm)
4	10¼" (26cm)	12¾" (32.4cm)
5	9" (22.9cm)	18¼" (46.4cm)
6	5½" (14cm)	22½" (57.2cm)
7	10½" (26.7cm)	25" (63.5cm)

Table 1

Step 5: Join the short ends of a bias strip back to itself using a bias seam (Figure 3). Press the seam allowance open and trim to a scant ¼" (6mm). Use the Basted Bias method to create a circle of bias approximately ¼" (6mm) wide. (Hint: This is a good time to use the free arm on a sewing machine!)

Step 6: Press the bias flat into a circle, and pin it in place over the traced lines on the background fabric. Starting with the inside edge, stitch along each folded edge (Figure 4).

Step 7: Press the quilt top. Baste the top together with the backing and batting. Quilt as desired. Watermark is quilted with circles echoing the appliqué.

Step 8: Bind with the 2½" (6.4cm) orange strips.

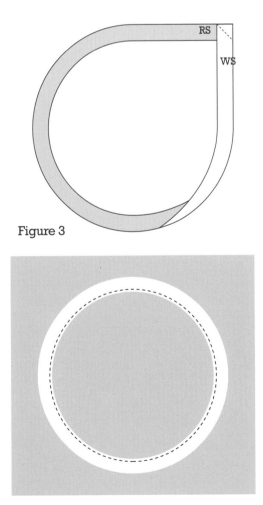

Figure 3

Figure 4

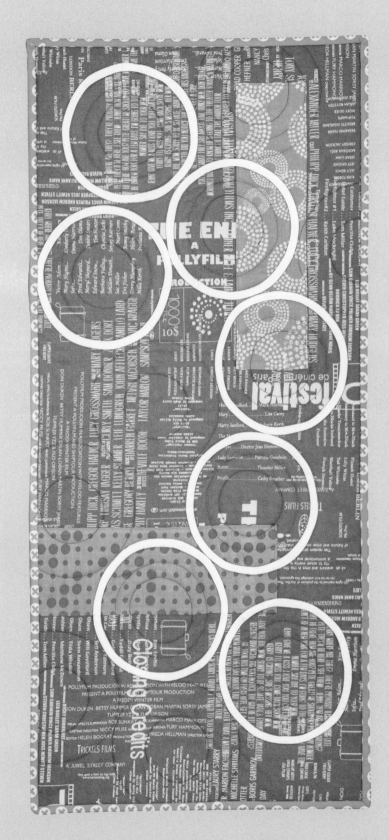

Forever

Finished size: 80" × 80" (203.2cm × 203.2cm)
Finished block: 12" (30.5cm)

I've always been drawn to designs that make secondary circle patterns. Forever was inspired by such classic quilt patterns as Double Wedding Ring and Orange Peel, as well as concrete blocks and an amazing ceiling. Rather than repeat the block over the entire quilt, I chose to give the quilt a worn feeling, like an old carving or engraving where time and use have dulled the pattern, but it can still be seen. The soft color scheme and use of the block design in the quilting reinforce the idea.

Fabric Requirements & Supplies

Background: 5¾ yards (5.3m)

Contrast and binding: 1¾ yards (1.6m)

Batting: 86" × 86" (218.4cm × 218.4cm)

Backing: 7⅓ yards (6.7m)

⅜" (1cm) bias tape maker

Removable pencil or marker

3–4 sheets of paper

Forever templates (see Templates)

Fabric Note

The fabrics used in this project are Robert Kaufman Kona Cotton Solids in Mustard and Snow.

Cutting Instructions

Background

Cut (12) 12½" (31.8cm) strips for the blocks.
Subcut (36) 12½" (31.8cm) squares.

Cut (4) 6½" (16.5cm) strips for the borders.

Cut (4) 2½" (6.4cm) strips for the borders.

Contrast

Cut (9) 2½" (6.4cm) strips for the binding.

Cut (2) ½ yard (0.5m) cuts for the bias strips. Subcut (45) ¾" (1.9cm) bias strips. Note: Follow the manufacturer's directions on the tapemaker if a width other than ¾" (1.9cm) is suggested.

Step 1: Trace each template twice onto regular paper. Match the top and bottom halves and tape them together. Match the left and right halves and tape them together (Figure 2).

Using a light box (or a window) and a removable marker or pencil, center a background block on top of the template and trace the design onto 15 background blocks. (A light box may not be needed if tracing on a light-colored surface with light background blocks.)

Step 2: Join 3 bias strips together diagonally on the short ends. Repeat with the remaining strips in sets of 3.

Using the manufacturer's instructions, make the bias strips into ⅜" (1cm) bias tape. It may be helpful to roll the finished bias tape onto a cardboard toilet paper roll or something similar.

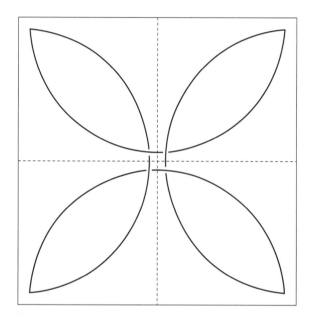

Figure 1

Weaving Bias Strips

Weaving bias strips under and over each other is traditional in bias appliqué. The template shows a continuous line for the over intersections and a broken line for under intersections (Figure 2).

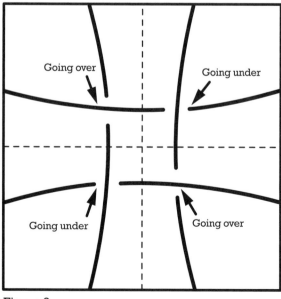

Figure 2

Step 3: Trim about 2" (5.1 cm) off the bias tape strip to avoid the join falling at a corner. Beginning at the center on an "under" spot and centering the bias tape over the traced lines, pin the bias tape in place on the background block. Pinning the bias in the direction indicated on the diagram will ensure the overs and unders flow easily (Figure 3).

Step 4: At the outside corners, fold the bias tape back on itself to turn the corner. Remember to weave the center overs and unders, and to finish up back at the beginning spot (Figure 4).

Step 5: Begin stitching on the inside curves first. Stitch close to the edge of the bias tape. Stitch the outer curves second. Repeat for 15 blocks (Figure 5).

Step 6: Lay out the applique blocks and the plain background blocks as shown in the quilt diagram on the following page. Sew the blocks into rows and the rows into the quilt top.

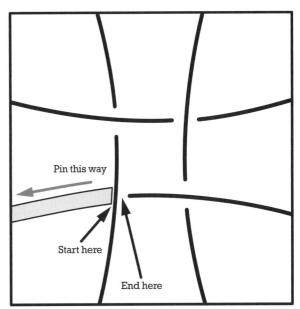

Figure 3

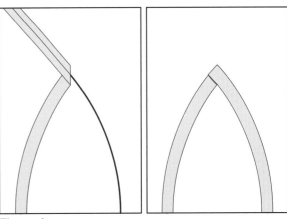

Figure 4

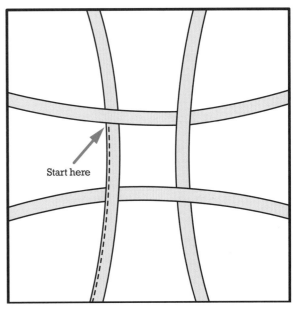

Figure 5

Step 7: Sew the 6½" (16.5cm) border strips together on the short ends and cut a 72½" (184.2cm) and an 80½" (204.5cm) piece.

Sew the 2½" (6.4cm) border strips together on the short ends and cut one 72½" (184.2cm) and one 80½" (204.5cm).

Sew the shorter 6½" (16.5cm) strip to the left side of the quilt top and the shorter 2½" (6.4cm) strip to the right side of the quilt top. Sew the longer 6½" (16.5cm) strip to the top of the quilt top and the longer 2½" (6.4cm) strip to the bottom of the quilt top (Figure 5).

Step 8: Press the quilt top. Baste the top together with the backing and batting. Quilt as desired. Forever is quilted in the ditch around the bias strips. The plain blocks are quilted with a design that echoes the bias blocks. A diamond was added in the center of the circles.

Step 9: Bind with the 2½" (6.4cm) contrast strips.

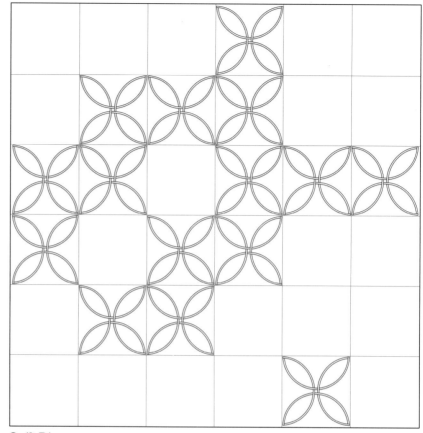

Quilt Diagram

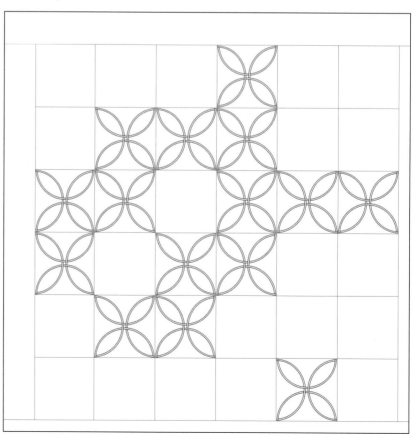

Figure 5

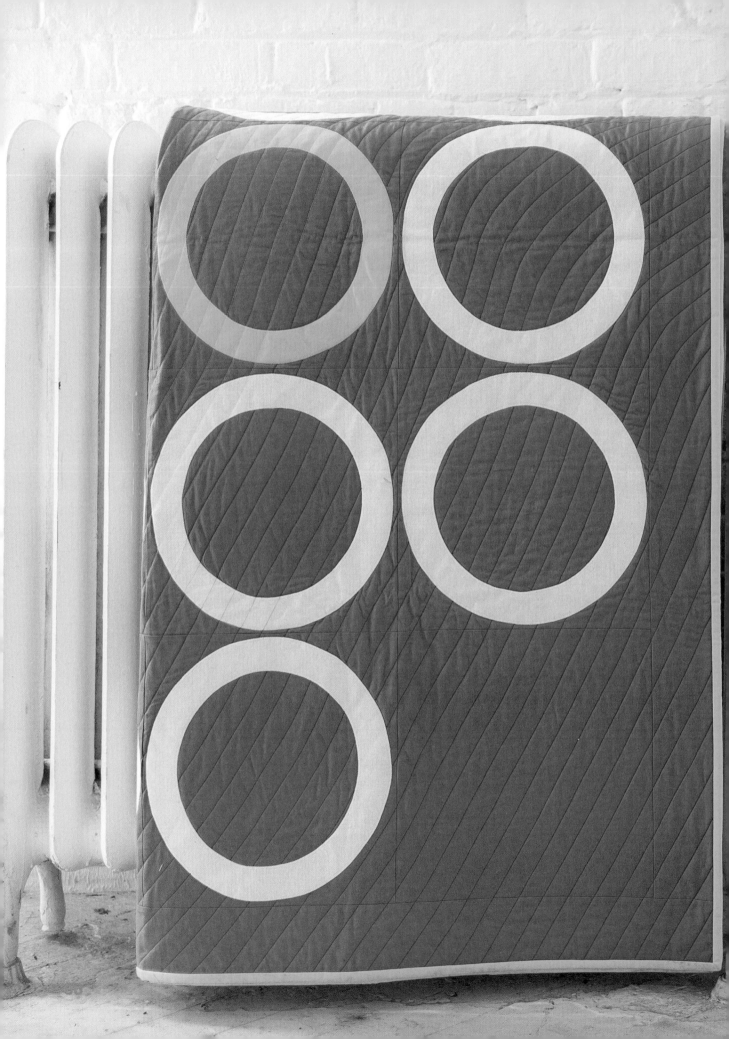

Road Work

Finished size: 66" × 66" (167.6cm × 167.6cm)
Finished block: 12" (30.5cm)

Often when I design quilts I start with a shape in mind. In this case it was a ring. After playing with colors and layouts, and settling on this one, it reminded me of those stacks of huge pipes you sometimes see during summer road construction season. I hope there is an invisible one in the bottom right corner and that the yellow one isn't the one they need first!

Fabric Requirements & Supplies

Background: 4¼ yards (3.9m)

Contrast (light): 2¼ yards (2.1m)

Accent and binding: 1 yard (0.9m)

Fusible web: 18" (45.7cm) wide, 5¾ yards (5.3m)

Stabilizer: 18" (45.7cm) wide, 5¾ yards (5.3m) (optional)

Batting: 72" × 72" (182.9cm × 182.9cm)

Backing: 4 yards (3.7m)

Circle template (see Templates)

Fabric Note
The fabrics used in this project are Robert Kaufman Kona Cotton Solids in Astral, White and Citrus.

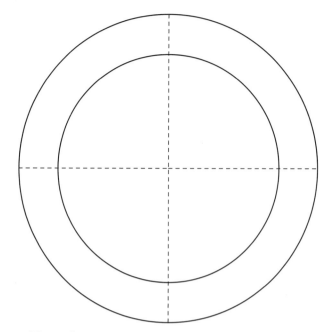

Figure 1

Step 1: Trace the circle pattern 4 times and tape the sections together to form a complete template. The diameter of the outer circle is 11½" (29.2cm) (Figure 1).

Step 2: Leaving approximately ½" (1.3cm) between each circle, trace 17 circles (including the lines marking the horizontal and vertical centers) onto the paper side of the fusible web. Number the circles as you trace them to avoid having to recount.

Following the manufacturer's directions for the fusible web, fuse 16 circles to the wrong side of the contrast fabric and 1 to the wrong side of the accent fabric. Cut out the circles on the inner and outer lines.

Step 3: Press 17 background blocks into 4 sections to mark the centers. Fuse the circles to the backgrounds, aligning the center marks and folds (Figure 2).

Using a zigzag stitch that is slightly more open than a satin stitch, stitch around the inner and outer circles with matching thread.

Step 4: Lay out the blocks according to the quilt diagram.

Sew the blocks into rows and the rows into the quilt top.

12½" (31.8cm)

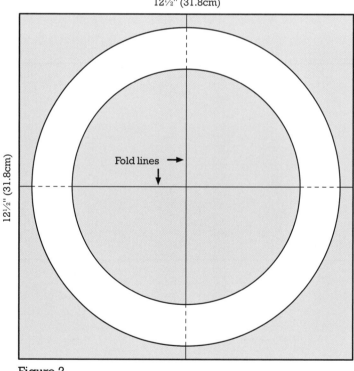

12½" (31.8cm)

Fold lines

Figure 2

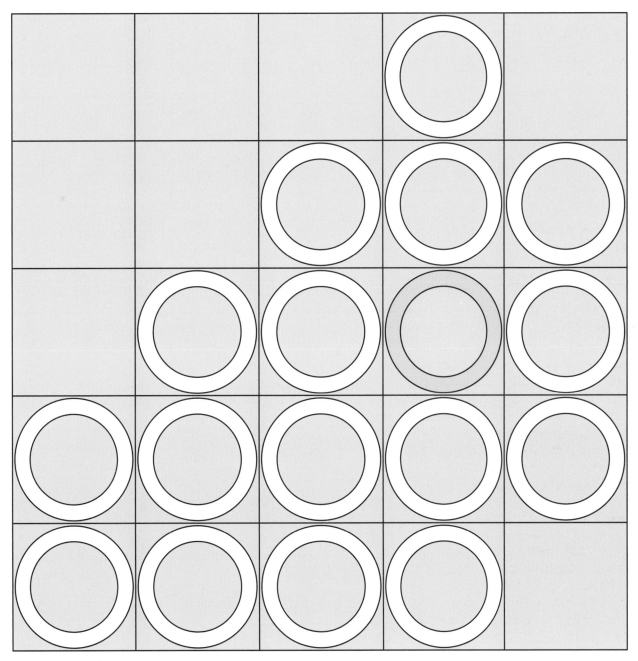

Quilt Diagram

Step 5: Sew the short ends of the 3½" (8.9cm) border strips together. Trim 2 to 60½" (153.7cm) and 2 to 66½" (168.9cm).

Sew the shorter strips to the sides of the quilt top and the longer strips to the top and bottom of the quilt top (Figure 3).

Step 6: Press the quilt top. Baste together with the backing and batting. Quilt as desired. Road Work is quilted with a "road" running from the top right to the bottom left of the quilt. The road itself is quilted in white with yellow accents and runs across the appliqué rings. The rest of the quilt is echo-quilted in blue and does not cross the appliqué.

Step 7: Bind with the 2½" (6.4cm) accent strips.

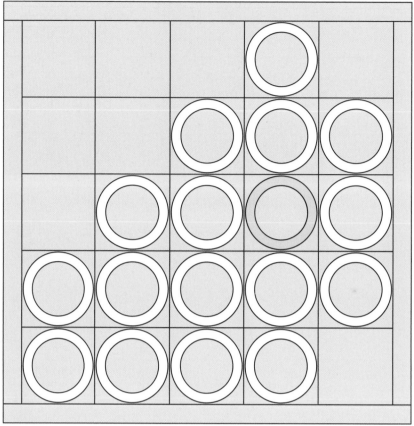

Figure 3

Chapter 6

Pictorial

I cannot draw at all. I understand now that drawing is a learned skill, but, when I was young I thought it was a talent you were either born with or not. Consequently, it was quite a thrill when I started using bias strips to draw with fabric. The fun fish in Deep Blue and the spare landscape of Community Isolation are both examples of bias-strip drawing. I have also now expanded my "drawing" to the traditional machine appliqué used in the darling tea cups of Cure-All and mid-mod houses of Clerestory.

Cure-All

Finished size: 30" × 30" (76.2cm × 76.2cm)
Finished block: 10" (25.4cm)

Raised by parents of Australian/English/Scottish descent, I've been a tea drinker all my life. Aside from drinking tea (with milk, please) on a daily basis, there has never been a crisis in my life that hasn't been improved by a cup of tea. Some crises have turned out to be, ahem, a tempest in a teapot. For the others, a cup of tea has at least helped me slow down and gain some perspective. I can't imagine life without the cure-all properties of a good cup of tea!

Fabric Requirements & Supplies

Background: 1 yard (0.9m)

Print for teacups: 5 fat eighths*

Binding: 1/3 yard (0.3m)

Batting: 36" × 36" (91.4cm × 91.4cm)

Backing: 1 1/8 yards (1m)

Fusible webbing: 1 1/4 yards (1.1m) of 18" (45.7cm) wide

Stabilizer (optional): 1 1/4 yards (1.1m) of 18" (45.7cm) wide

Teacup template

*A fat eighth measures 9" × 22" (22.9cm × 55.9cm)

Fabric Note
The background fabric used in this project is Grunge by Basic Gray for Moda. The tea cups are Liberty of London Tana Lawn.

Cutting Instructions

Background

Cut (3) 10½" strips. Subcut (9)
10½" (26.7cm) squares.

Binding

Cut (3) 2½" (6.4cm) strips.

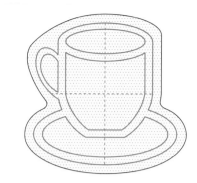

Figure 1

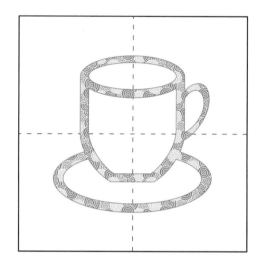

Figure 2

Step 1: Fold the background blocks in half vertically and horizontally and press it to mark the centers.

Step 2: Trace the teacup template and center markings onto the fusible webbing 9 times. Cut out around the template, leaving approximately ¼" (6mm) from the outer traced lines (Figure 1).

Fuse 2 teacups to the wrong side of 4 of the fabrics and 1 to the 5th fabric. Cut out on the lines including inside the rim, handle, cup and saucer.

Step 3: Matching the center of the teacup to the centers on the background block, fuse the appliqué onto the background (Figure 2).

Step 4: Pin the stablizer under the block and stitch the appliqué in place using an open zigzag stitch. Repeat for 9 blocks.

Step 5: Sew the blocks into 3 rows of 3 blocks and then the 3 rows into the quilt top.

Step 6: Press the quilt top. Baste together with the backing and batting. Quilt as desired. Cure-All is quilted with a free motion watery design.

Step 7: Bind with the 2½" (6.4cm) strips.

Quilt Diagram

Clerestory

Finished size: 64" × 74" (162.6cm × 188cm)
Finished block: 10" × 15" (25.4cm × 38.1cm) finished

House quilts have always been among my favorite quilts and I was pretty excited about the mid-century modern inspired sketch that became Clerestory. Translating quilt sketches into actual quilt parts and instructions can be quite a challenge. The piecing instructions for the bottom half of this house were easy, but the roof was quite uncooperative. After experimenting with traditional piecing, paper piecing and appliqué, I chose appliqué as the easiest and most fabric-saving way to complete the block.

The color scheme for this quilt was inspired by the Mezzanine print of Cotton + Steel August by Sarah Watts. I fell in love with the fabric and the aqua, navy and curry combination so I pulled those colors out of the print and used them to complete the quilt. I don't often use this method of color selection, but I'm thrilled with the results.

Fabric Requirements & Supplies

Background: 4¾ yards (4.3m)

Print 1 (blocks and binding): 1 yard (0.9m)

Print 2: ⅓ yard (0.3m)

Green solid: ⅓ yard (0.3m)

Curry solid: ½ yard (0.5m)

Navy solid: ½ yard (0.5m)

Batting: 70" × 80" (177.8cm × 203.2cm)

Backing: 4 yards (3.7m)

Fusible web: 2 yards (1.8m)

Stabilizer (optional): 2 yards (1.8)

Roof template (see Templates)

Fabric Note
The fabrics used in this project were Mezzanine and Diamond from Cotton + Steel August by Sarah Watts and Robert Kaufman Kona Cotton Solids in Candy Green, Navy and Curry.

Cutting Instructions

Note: I like to keep my pieces organized by letter in plastic baggies.

Blocks: Print 1, Print 2, Green solid

Cut a 10" (25.4cm) WOF strip. Subcut (1) 16" (40.6cm) Z piece for the appliqué. Cut the remaining piece into 1" (2.5cm) strips and subcut into (4) 12¾" (32.4cm) Y pieces, (8) 6½" (16.5cm) W pieces, (8) 4½" (11.4cm) X pieces, (8) 4" (10.2cm) T pieces, (4) 2½" (6.4cm) U pieces and (8) 1½" (3.8cm) V pieces.

Blocks: Navy and Curry solids

Cut (1) 12" (30.5cm) WOF strip. Cut a 16" (40.6cm) Z piece for the appliqué. Cut the remaining piece into 1" (2.5cm) strips and subcut

in (6) 12¾" (32.4cm) Y pieces, (12) 6½" (16.5cm) W pieces, (12) 4½" (11.4cm) X pieces, (12) 4" (10.2cm) T pieces, (6) 2½" (6.4cm) U pieces and (12) 1½" (3.8cm) V pieces.

Background

Cut (4) 14½" (36.8cm) strips. Subcut (24) 5½" × 14½" (14cm × 36.8cm) G pieces.

Cut (2) 10½" (26.7cm) strips. Subcut (4) 10½" × 15½" (26.7cm × 39.4cm) pieces for the "blank" blocks.

Cut (11) 2½" (6.4cm) strips; set 7 aside for the borders. Subcut the rest into (24) 6½" (16.5cm) D pieces.

Cut (3) 2¼" (5.7cm) strips. Subcut into (24) 5" (12.7cm) F pieces.

Cut (6) 1¾" (4.4cm) strips. Subcut into (48) 4½" (11.4cm) A pieces.

Cut (6) 1½" (3.8cm) strips. Subcut into (24) 5½" (14cm) C pieces and (24) 4" (10.2cm) B pieces.

Cut (3) 1¼" (3.2cm) strips. Subcut into (24) 4½" (11.4cm) E pieces.

Cut (24) 1" (2.5cm) strips. Subcut into (24) 15½" (39.4cm) I pieces and (48) 10" (25.4cm) H pieces.

Binding: Print 1

Cut (8) 2½" (6.4cm) strips.

NOTE: Use the same house fabric for each piece in each block. There will be 4 blocks each in Print 1, Print 2 and the green solid, and 6 each in the navy and curry solids for 24 houses total. Always press away from the background unless noted otherwise.

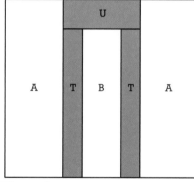

Figure 1
Door section

Step 1: Sew 2 T pieces on either side of piece B. Sew piece U to the top of this unit. Sew an A piece to each side of this unit to complete the door section. (Figure 1).

Step 2: Sew the V pieces to each short side of piece C. Sew the W pieces to the top and bottom of this unit. Sew piece D to the bottom of the unit and then E to the right side to complete the window section (Figure 2).

Sew the window section to the right side of the door section.

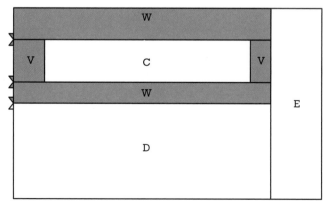

Figure 2
Window section

Step 3: Add the walls: Sew an X piece to each side of the window/door section. Sew piece Y to the bottom of the unit. Sew piece F to the right side of this unit (Figure 3).

Step 4: Sew piece G to the top of the Wall unit.

Trace both sections of the roof pattern onto regular paper and tape them together along the dashed line to make the roof template. Trace the roof template onto the paper side of the fusible web, nesting to fit the Z pieces of fabric (Figure 4).

Trace 3 sets of 4 roof patterns to fit in a 10" × 16" (25.4cm × 40.6cm) piece of fabric (Z for prints and green) and 2 sets of 6 roof patterns to fit a 12" × 16" (30.5cm × 40.6cm) piece of fabric (Z for navy and curry).

Step 5: Fuse the sets of roof patterns to the wrong side of the fabric and cut them out on the traced lines.

Step 6: Place the roof appliqué so that the lower edges of the roof meet the inside corners of the outer walls (Figure 5). Fuse in place. Stitch along the upper and lower raw edges of the roof using matching thread and a slightly open zigzag stitch.

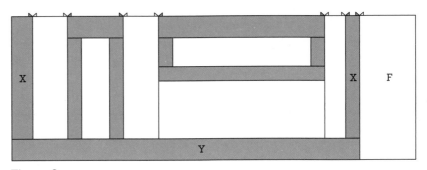

Figure 3
Wall unit

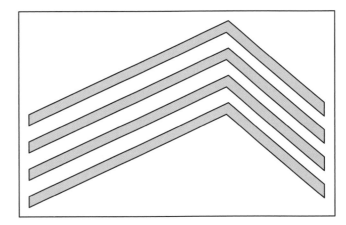

Figure 4

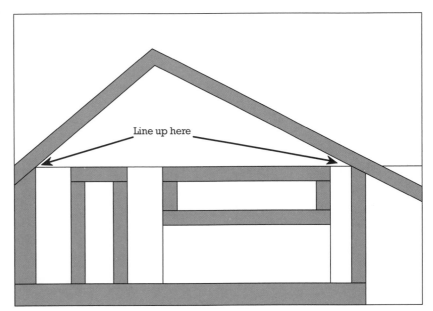

Figure 5

Step 7: Sew piece H to both sides of the house unit and piece I to the bottom to complete the block (Figure 6). Press toward the H and I pieces.

Make 4 blocks each using the 2 prints and the green solid. Make 6 blocks each of the navy and curry solids.

Step 8: Lay out the blocks in 7 rows of 4, adding in the 4 blank blocks according to the quilt diagram. Sew the blocks into rows and the rows into the quilt top center.

Step 9: Sew the short ends of the seven 2½" (6.4cm) strips set aside for the borders together. Trim 2 to 64½" (163.8cm) and 2 to 70½" (179.1cm). Sew the longer strips to the sides of the quilt top and the shorter strips to the top and bottom.

Step 10: Press the quilt top. Baste the top together with the backing and batting. Quilt as desired. Clerestory is quilted with horizontal lines spaced every inch (2.5cm) and vertical lines spaced every 5" (12.7cm). This echoes the shape of the clerestory window in the block.

Step 11: Bind with the 2½" (6.4cm) strips.

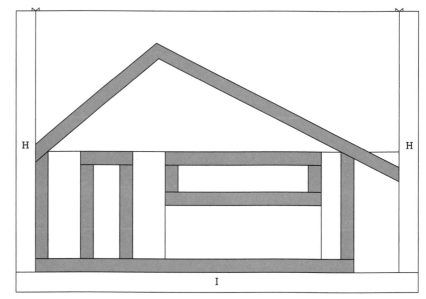

Figure 6

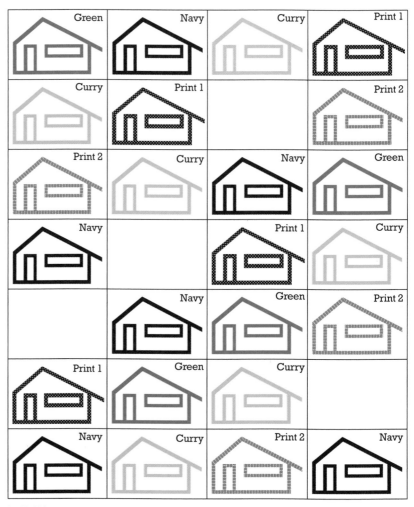

Quilt Diagram

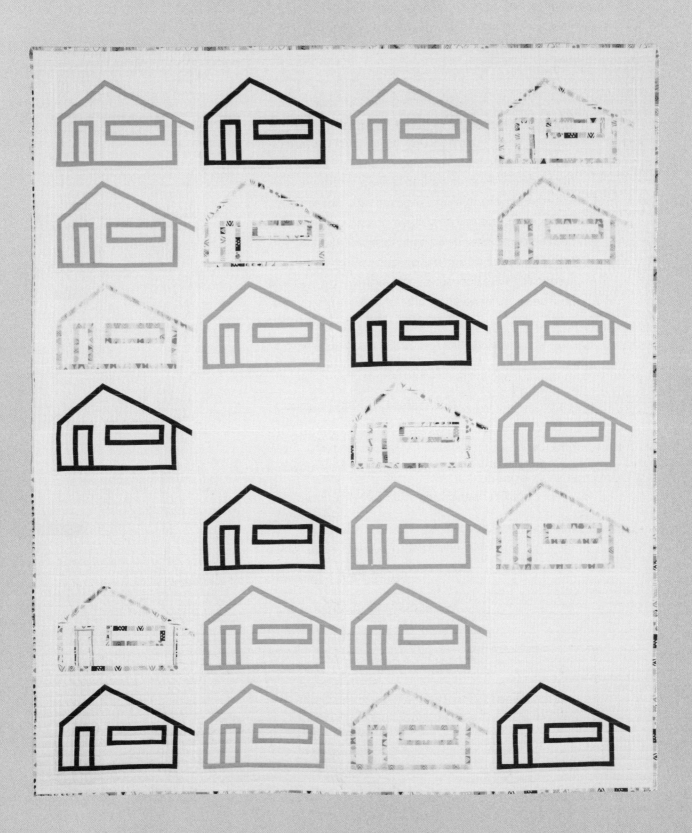

Deep Blue

Finished size: 36" × 45" (91.4cm × 114.3cm)

What is more relaxing and fun than a beautiful tropical blue sea and lots of brightly colored fish? Whether this quilt is a gift for a special child or a wall hanging to remind you of warmer days, it is sure to make you smile.

Fabric Requirements & Supplies

Background: 1½ yards (1.4m)

Fish: 4–8 bright fat quarters* or 15" (38.1cm) squares for small fish

Large fish (silver): 1 fat quarter*

Waterline and binding (dark blue): ⅞ yard (0.8m)

Batting: 42" × 51" (106.7cm × 129.5cm)

Backing: 1½ yards (1.4m)

Removable marking pencil

½ yard (0.5m) freezer paper

¼" (6mm) and ⅜" (1cm) bias tape maker

Fish and waterline templates (see Templates)

*A fat quarter measures 18" × 22" (45.7cm × 55.9cm)

Fabric Note

The fabrics used in this project are Robert Kaufman Kona Cotton Solids in Jamaica (background), Lagoon (waterline and binding), Chinese Red, Flame, Citrus, Pomegranate, Parrot, Riviera, Purple and Silver.

Cutting Instructions

Background

Cut a 45½" (115.6cm) strip and trim to 36½" × 45½" (92.7cm × 115.6cm) piece.

Waterline and Binding

Cut (5) 2½" (6.4cm) strips for the binding.

From the remaining fabric, cut (2) ¾" (1.9cm) bias strips (or whatever width suggested by the ⅜" [1cm] bias tape maker manufacturer).

Small fish

Cut 1 bias strip ½" (1.3cm) wide (or whatever width suggested by the ¼" [6mm] bias tape maker manufacturer) for each fish from the centers of the fat quarters or squares. Cut a total of 8 bias strips.

Large fish

Cut 2 bias strips ½" (1.3cm) wide (or whatever width suggested by the ¼" [6mm] bias tape maker manufacturer) from the center of the silver fat quarter.

Step 1: Join the bias strips for the waterline using a bias seam, pressing it open. Use the ⅜" (1cm) bias tape maker to make bias tape.

Step 2: Fold the top of the background down 12" (30.5cm) and lightly press the fold.

Step 3: Cut 2 strips of freezer paper each about 4" (10.2cm) wide. Tape them together on the short ends and trace the waterline template onto the freezer paper 3 to 4 times. Cut out along 1 side of the traced line.

Step 4: Place the freezer paper onto the background fabric with the bottom of the waterline waves touching the pressed line. Using the removable pencil, trace along the edge of the freezer paper (Figure 1).

Centering the bias tape over the line, pin it in place. Straight stitch along each edge of the bias tape.

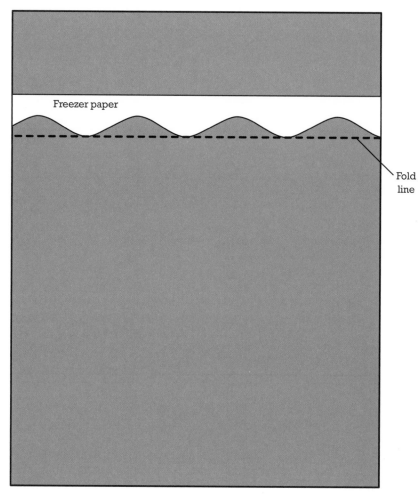

Figure 1

Step 5: Using the fish patterns, trace 2 or 3 small fish and 1 large fish onto the freezer paper. Cut out on the traced lines leaving a little extra where the tail and body meet to keep them connected.

Step 6: Using the removable pencil, mark dots on the background fabric at the intersections listed in Table 1. These mark the nose and top edge of the tail of each fish.

Step 7: Using a dry iron, press the freezer paper templates in place, matching the nose and top of tail dots. Place a ruler along the fish belly and tail and line it up it with the edge of the background fabric to make sure the fish are straight. Trace around the templates, sketching the tail/body connection as needed.

Step 8: Using the ¼" (6mm) bias tape maker, make bias tape from the strips cut for the small fish.

Begin with the raw edge of the bias at the intersection of the body and tail. Centering the bias over the traced line on the background and folding the bias back on itself at the nose and tail, pin the bias in place. (See Figure 4 on page 93.) The raw edges should be covered by the bias crossing at the body/tail join (Figure 2).

Begin stitching along the edge of the bias on the inside of the fish body first. Stitch the other edge of the bias. Repeat for 7 more small fish. Note that fish 3 is facing the opposite way from the rest of the fish.

Step 9: Join the bias strips for the large fish using a bias seam. Press the seam. Use the ¼"(6mm) bias tape maker to make bias tape.

Continue in the same manner as you did for the small fish in Step 4.

Fish	Nose		Top of Tail		Color
	from top raw edge	from left raw edge	from top raw edge	from left raw edge	color used in project shown
1	17¼" (43.8cm)	3¾" (9.5cm)	16" (40.6cm)	9¾" (24.8cm)	orange
2	16¾" (42.5cm)	23¼" (59.1cm)	15½" (39.4cm)	29¼" (74.3cm)	purple
3	22¼" (56.5cm)	16¾" (42.5cm)	21" (53.3cm)	10¾" (27.3cm)	white
4	25¾" (65.4cm)	24½" (62.2cm)	24½" (62.3cm)	30½" (77.5cm)	pink
5	27¾" (70.5cm)	14½" (36.8cm)	26½" (67.3cm)	20½" (52.1cm)	yellow
6	32¼" (81.9cm)	4¼" (10.8cm)	31" (78.7cm)	10¼" (26cm)	red
7	34¼" (87cm)	19" (48.3cm)	33" (83.8cm)	25" (63.5cm)	green
8	39¾" (101cm)	25¼" (64.1cm)	38½" (98.8cm)	31¼" (79.4cm)	blue
9	41" (104.1cm)	6¼" (15.9cm)	39¼" (99.7cm)	20¼" (51.4cm)	silver

Table 1

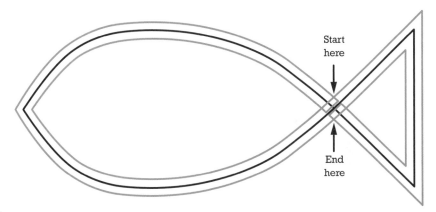

Figure 2

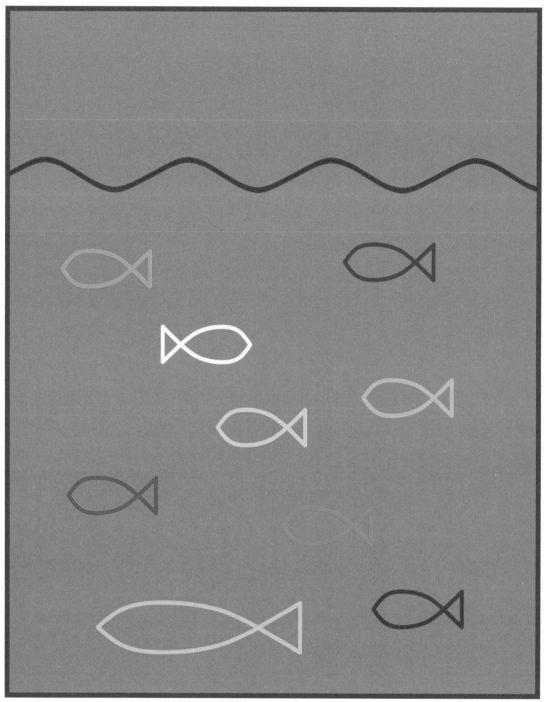

Quilt Diagram

Step 10: Press the quilt top. Baste the top together with the backing and batting. Quilt as desired. Deep Blue is quilted with random wavy lines in the water and soft curved lines to represent a breeze stitched in the sky.

Step 11: Bind with the 2½" (6.4cm) strips.

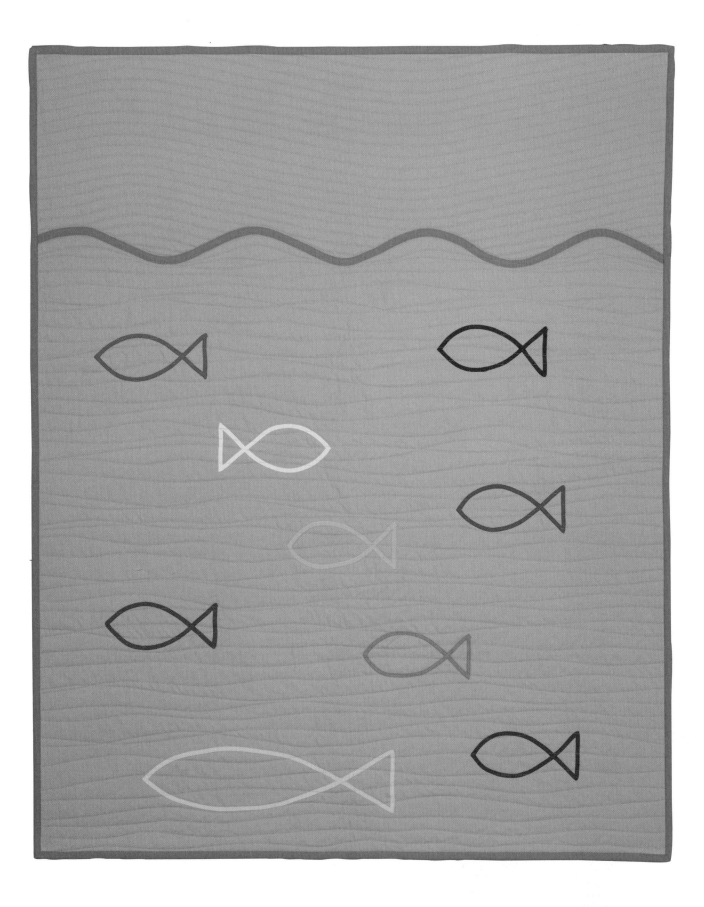

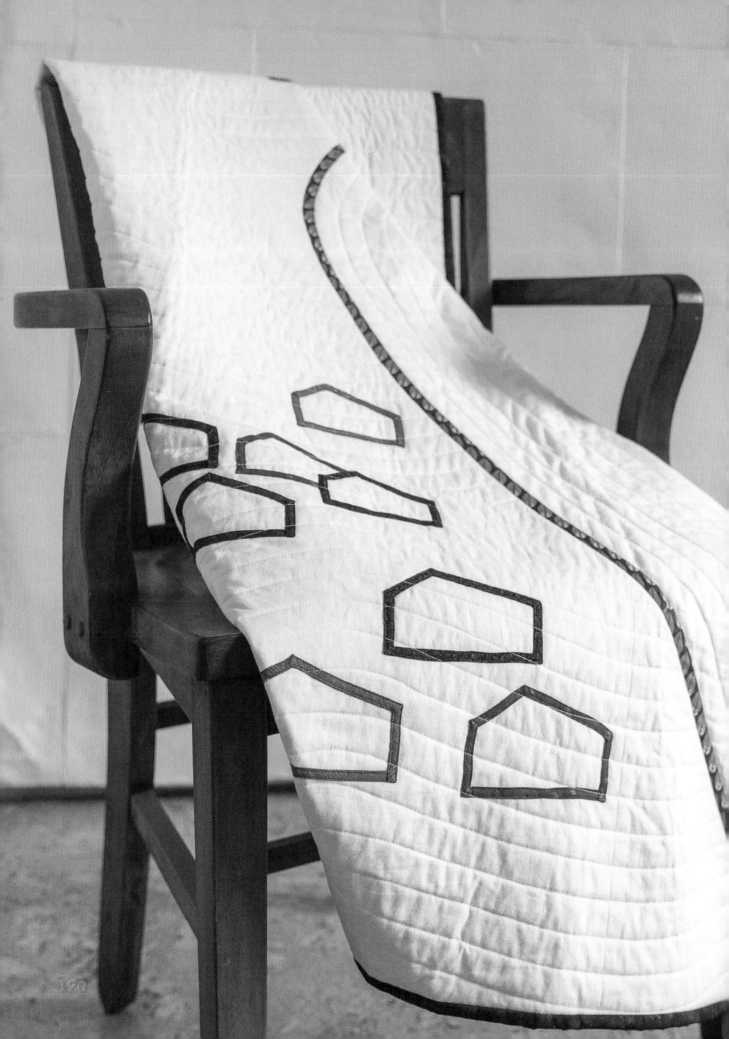

Community Isolation

Finished size: 50" × 50" (127cm × 127cm)

This quilt was inspired by the novel *South of Superior* by Ellen Airgood. The story takes place in a small town on the shores of Lake Superior in Michigan's Upper Peninsula. The novel spoke to me about the ways we perceive community and isolation in the context of the people and places in our lives.

Fabric Requirements & Supplies

Background: $2\frac{1}{4}$ yards (2.1m)

Shoreline (blue): 1 fat quarter

Trees (green): (6) 13" (33cm) squares

Houses (neutral): (5) 12" (30.5cm) squares

Binding: $\frac{1}{2}$ yard (0.5m)

Batting: 56" × 56" (142.3cm × 142.3cm)

Backing: $3\frac{1}{4}$ yards (3m)

Removable marking pencil

$\frac{1}{4}$–$\frac{1}{2}$ yard (0.2–.05m) freezer paper

$\frac{1}{2}$" (1.3cm) bias tape maker

Stabilizer (optional): $\frac{1}{4}$–$\frac{1}{2}$ yard (0.2–0.5m)

House and tree templates

Fabric Note

The background fabric used in this project is Cross Section in White from Doe by Carolyn Friedlander for Robert Kaufman.

Cutting Instructions

Background

Cut a 50½" (128.3cm) strip. Subcut to 41" (104.1cm).

Cut (2) 10½" (26.7cm) strips.

Shoreline

Cut (3) 1" (2.5cm) bias strips from the center of the fat quarter.

Trees

Cut (1) ¾" (1.9cm) bias strip from the center of each of the 13" (33cm) squares.

Houses

Cut (1) ¾" (1.9cm) bias strip from the center of each of the 12" (30.5cm) squares.

Binding

Cut (6) 2½" (6.4cm) strips.

Step 1: Sew the two 10½" (26.7cm) background strips together on the short ends and trim the length to 50½" (128.3cm). Using a ½" (1.3cm) seam, sew this piece to the long side of the 50½" (128.3cm) background strip to make a 50½" (128.3cm) square. Press the seam open.

Step 2: For the shoreline, sew the short ends of the bias strips together using a bias seam. Press the seams open. Using the ½" (1.3cm) bias tape maker, make a bias strip at least 68" (172.7cm) long. Press.

Step 3: Using Table 1 and a removable marking pencil, mark dots at the intersections listed. Pin the bias tape from dot to dot, smoothing the curve (Figure 1). Creating a smooth curve is much more important than hitting the dots exactly. Stitch the inside curve (the lake side) along the edge first, then stitch the other edge.

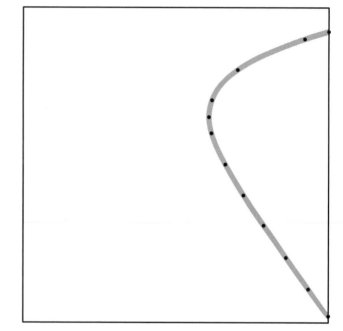

Figure 1

Distance from top edge	Distance from right edge
4" (10.2cm)	n/a
5" (12.7cm)	4" (10.2cm)
10" (25.4cm)	15" (38.1cm)
15" (38.1cm)	19" (48.3cm)
17½" (44.5cm)	20" (50.8cm)
20" (50.8cm)	19¼" (48.9cm)
25" (63.5cm)	17" (43.2cm)
30" (76.2cm)	14" (35.6cm)
35" (88.9cm)	11" (27.9cm)
40" (101.6cm)	7" (17.8cm)
45" (114.3cm)	3¼" (8.3cm)
49½" (125.7cm)	n/a

Table 1

Step 4: Trace the tree and house patterns onto the freezer paper, and cut out using the traced lines as guides.

Using Table 2 for the trees and Table 3 for the houses, place the lower left corner of the freezer paper shapes at the coordinates listed. Using a dry iron, press the shapes in place. Trace around the shapes.

Step 5: To appliqué the trees, trim 5 of the 6 strips to 16½" (41.9cm); set the sixth strip aside. Using a bias seam, sew the short ends of each strip together to form a loop, and press the seam open. Use the Basting Method to make bias tape approximately ¼" (6mm) wide. Press. Basting near the seam can be tricky so add a pin or two to keep the edges in place.

Use the sixth strip and the Basting Method to make a bias strip approximately ¼" (6mm) wide for Tree 2. Press.

Tree	Distance from top edge	Distance from left edge
1	13" (33cm)	3½" (8.9cm)
2	13¼" (33.7cm)	8¾" (22.2cm)
3	17" (43.2cm)	7" (17.8cm)
4	15½" (39.4cm)	10½" (26.7cm)
5	24½" (62.2cm)	4¾" (12.1cm)
6	22½" (57.2cm)	9½" (24.1cm)

Table 2

House	Size	Distance from top edge	Distance from right edge
1	S	5¾" (14.6cm)	10½" (26.7cm)
2	S	11" (27.9cm)	21¾" (55.2cm)
3	M	29¾" (75.6cm)	20¼" (51.4cm)
4	M	33¾" (85.7cm)	27¼" (69.2cm)
5	M	34" (86.4cm)	22½" (57.2cm)
6	M	34¾" (88.3cm)	19¾" (50.2cm)
7	M	36½" (92.7cm)	24¾" (62.9cm)
8	L	40¼" (102.2cm)	18" (45.7cm)
9	L	43¾" (111.1cm)	22¼" (56.5cm)
10	L	44" (111.8cm)	15¼" (38.7cm)

Table 3

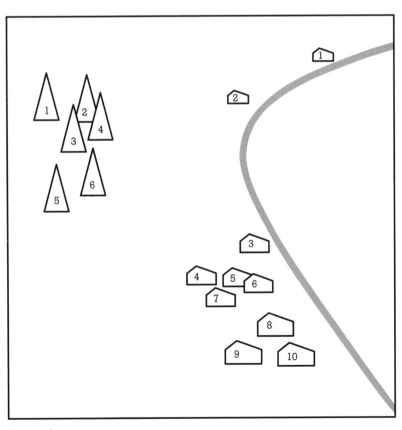

Figure 2

Step 6: Begin with Tree 2, as its corners are covered by Trees 3 and 4. Cut a 2½" (6.4cm) piece from the bias strip and center it over the traced line on the bottom of Tree 2. Trim the ends where they touch the lines for Trees 3 and 4. Stitch in place.

Use the rest of the strip to make the top part of the tree, folding the strip on itself to make the tip and then trimming again where the strip touches the lines for Trees 3 and 4. Stitch in place (Figure 3).

Step 7: Starting with Tree 1 and placing the seam on the bottom edge of the tree, center and pin the strip over the traced line, folding the strip on itself to turn the corners. Stitch in place (Figure 4).

Repeat for Trees 3–6, making sure that Trees 3 and 4 cover the raw edges of Tree 2.

Step 8: For the large houses (8–10), trim the 3 bias strips to 15¼" (38.7cm) long. Using a bias seam, sew the short ends of each strip together to form a loop. Press the seam open. Use the Basting Method to make bias tape approximately ¼" (6mm) wide. Press.

Placing the seam along the bottom edge of the house, center the strip over the traced line, folding the strip on itself to turn the corners and to form the roof. Pin the house in place and stitch along each edge (Figure 5).

Tips for Easier Stitching

Make all of the folds face the same direction.
Use a walking foot to stitch.
Use stabilizer.

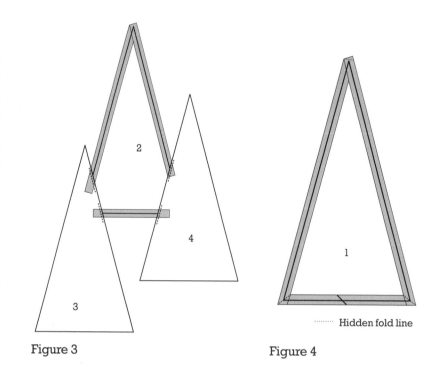

Figure 3

·········· Hidden fold line

Figure 4

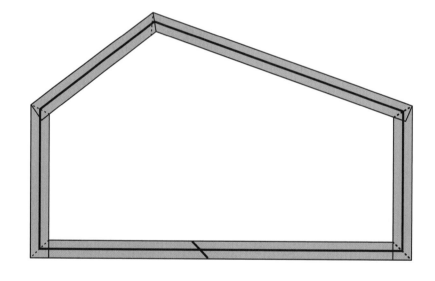

·········· Hidden fold line

Figure 5

Quilt Diagram

Step 9: For the medium houses (3–7), trim 4 strips to 12¾" (32.4cm); set the fifth strip aside. Using a bias seam, sew the short ends of each strip together to form a loop, pressing the seam open. Use the Basting Method to make bias tape approximately ¼" (6mm) wide. Press.

Use the fifth strip and the Basting Method to make a bias strip approximately ¼" (6mm) wide for House 5. Press.

Begin with the straight strip for House 5, as its corner is covered by House 6. Beginning where the roof of House 5 touches the roof of House 6, pin the strip in place over the traced line. Finish pinning where the bottom edge of House 5 touches the wall of House 6. Trim the edge of the strip even with the traced line of House 6. Stitch in place along each edge.

For Houses 3–4 and 6–7, placing the seam along the bottom edge of the house, center the strip over the traced line and pin in place. Stitch along each edge, making sure that the strip for House 6 covers the raw edges of House 5.

Step 10: For the small houses (1–2), trim 2 strips to 9½" (24.1cm) long. Using a bias seam, sew the short ends of each strip together to form a loop, pressing the seam open. Use the Basting Method to make bias tape approximately ¼" (6mm) wide. Press. Placing the seam along the bottom edge of the house, center the strip over the traced line and pin it in place. Stitch along each edge.

Step 11: Press the quilt top. Baste the top together with the backing and batting. Quilt as desired. Community Isolation is quilted with landscape-like curves to represent rolling hills and the water.

Step 12: Bind with the 2½"(6.4cm) strips.

Templates

Facets
Template shown at 100%

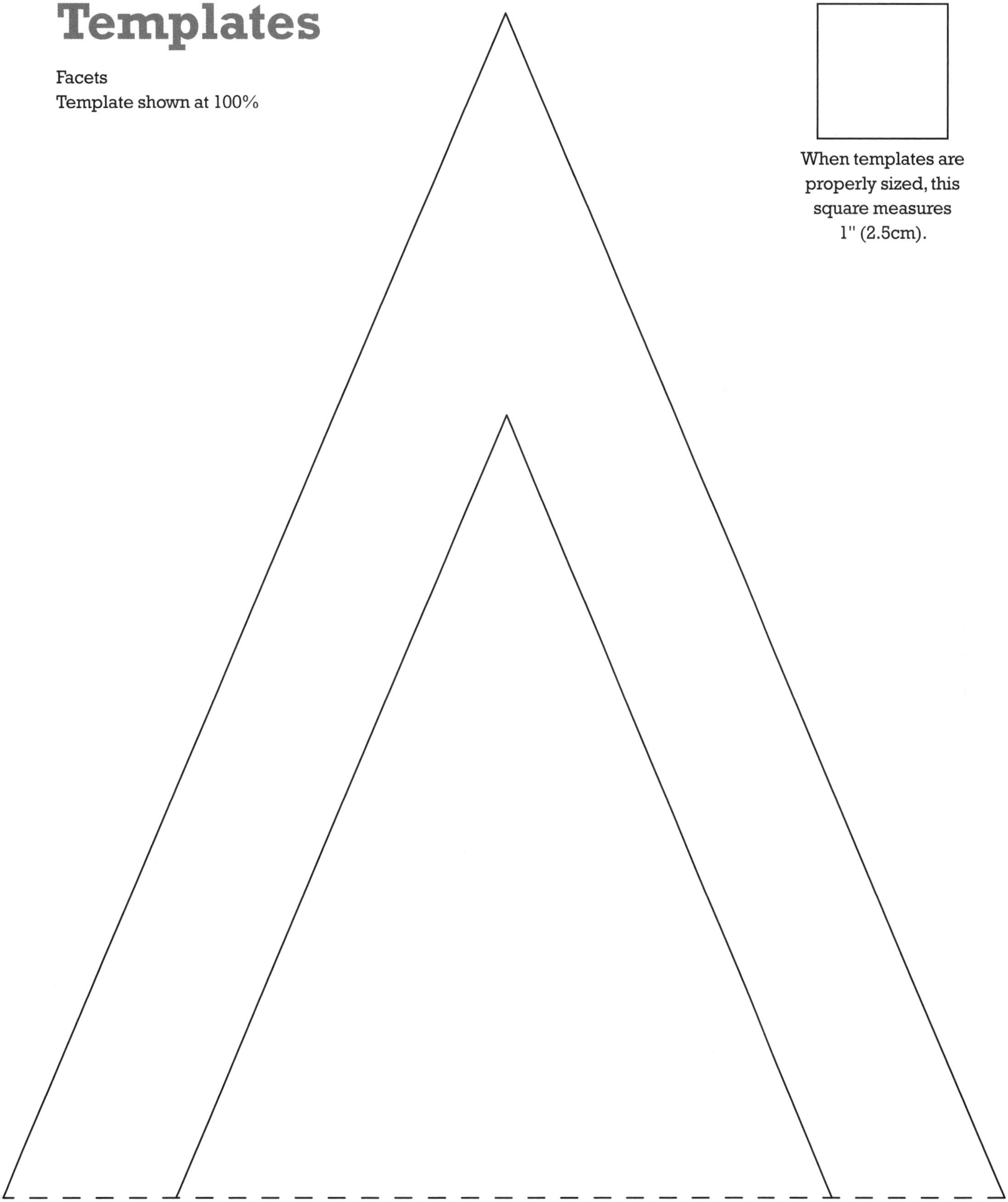

When templates are
properly sized, this
square measures
1" (2.5cm).

Templates

Clerestory
Template shown at 100%

When templates are
properly sized, this
square measures
1" (2.5cm).

Roof
Piece A

Templates

Clerestory
Template shown at 100%

When templates are
properly sized, this
square measures
1" (2.5cm).

Roof
Piece B

Templates

Community Isolation
Template shown at 100%

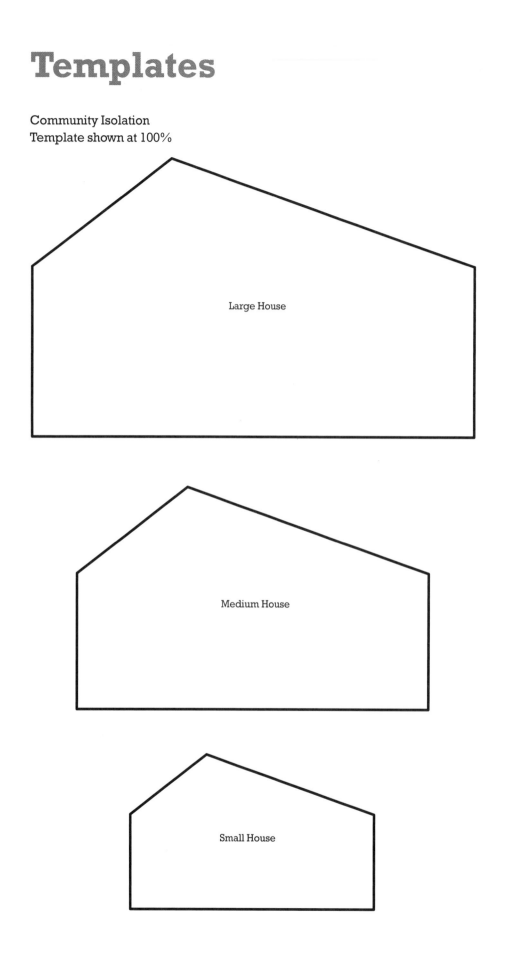

Large House

Medium House

Small House

When templates are properly sized, this square measures 1" (2.5cm).

Templates

Community Isolation
Template shown at 100%

When templates are properly sized, this square measures 1" (2.5cm).

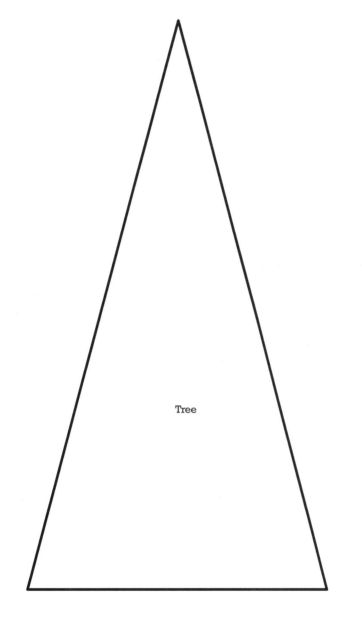

Tree

Templates

Deep Blue
Template shown at 100%

When templates are properly sized, this square measures 1" (2.5cm).

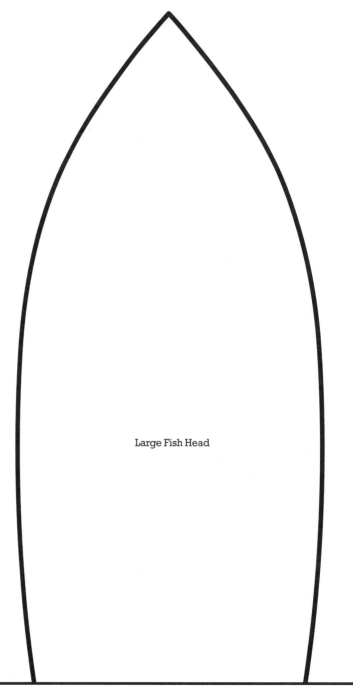

Large Fish Head

Templates

Deep Blue
Template shown at 100%

When templates are
properly sized, this
square measures
1" (2.5cm).

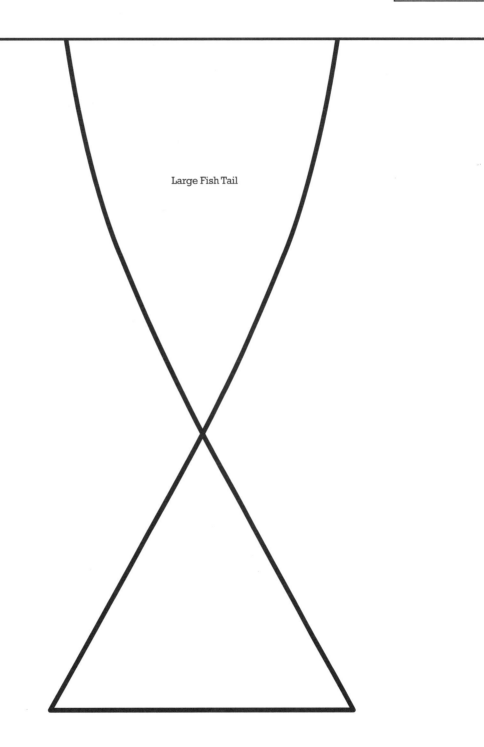

Large Fish Tail

Templates

Deep Blue
Templates shown at 100%

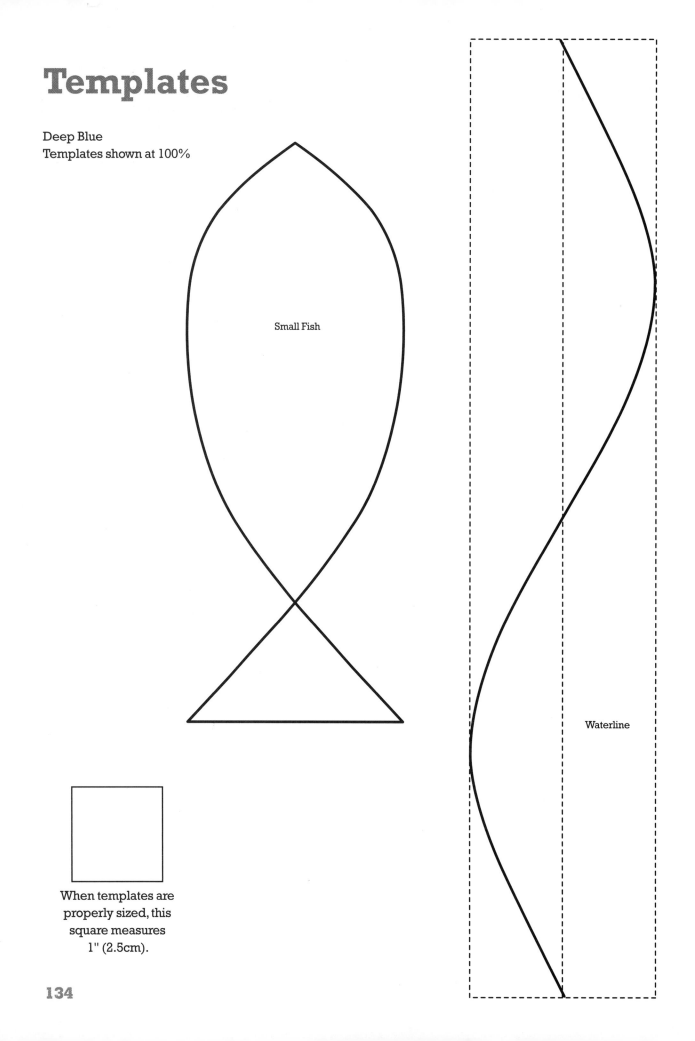

Small Fish

Waterline

When templates are
properly sized, this
square measures
1" (2.5cm).

Templates

Molecule
Template shown at 100%

When templates are
properly sized, this
square measures
1" (2.5cm).

Top

Templates

Forever
Template shown at 100%

When templates are
properly sized, this
square measures
1" (2.5cm).

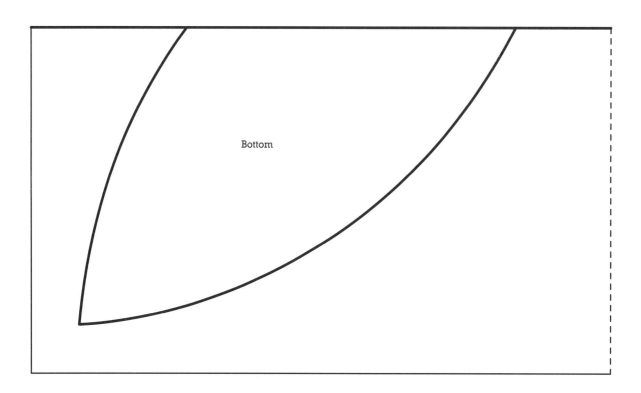

Bottom

Templates

Forever
Template shown at 100%

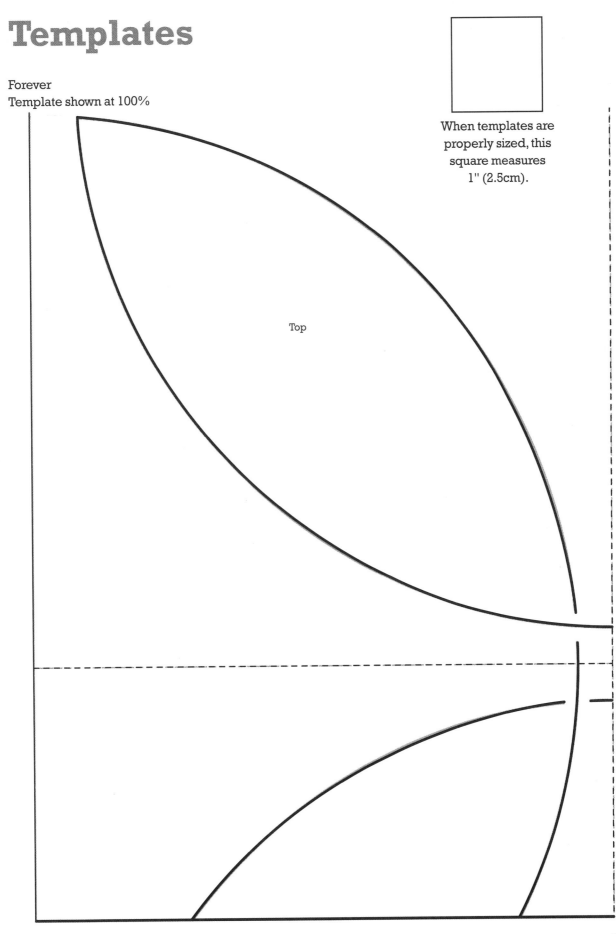

Top

When templates are
properly sized, this
square measures
1" (2.5cm).

Templates

Road Work
Template shown at 100%

When templates are
properly sized, this
square measures
1" (2.5cm).

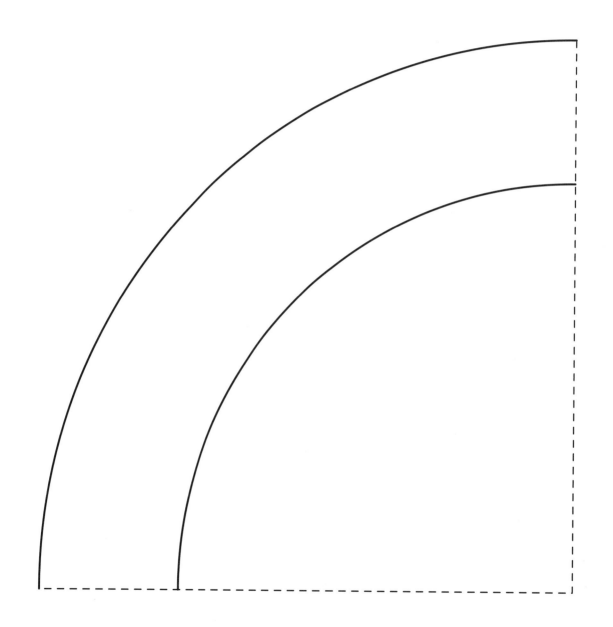

Templates

Watermark
Template shown at 100%

Templates

Cure-All
Template shown at 100%

When templates are
properly sized, this
square measures
1" (2.5cm).

Index

Dedication

For Mike, whose unwavering faith that I can do anything I set my mind to keeps me going when I'm not sure I can. All my love, Debbie

Acknowledgments

Thank you to all who provided so much encouragement to me through the process of writing this book. Thank you to the wonderful team at F+W/Fons & Porter, especially Amelia Johanson and Stephanie White. Thank you to Sue Friend for her ability to turn my sketches into wonderful illustrations and diagrams.

Thanks to my family and friends, especially Misha and Heather. I don't know if there is a greater gift than for your children to be enthusiastic about and proud of the work you do.

Special thanks to the members of my Handwork group: Marilyn Agin, Sharon Bell, Judy Endres, Sue Endreszl, Margaret Harris and Renee Panther, several of whom made quilt tops for this book. These wonderful women have taught me so much more than quilting over the past eight or so years, and I am a richer person for knowing them.

Thanks also to Hayley Cason and Kathy Koch for their sewing and quilting efforts.

I am honored to be a part of this wonderful quilting industry, with many members who so graciously and generously share their knowledge, experience and ideas.

Finally, thanks to my husband, Mike, my mother, Barbara Dunn, and the dearest and truest of friends, Susan Greenlee.

Photo by Heather Grikfa

About the Author

After a lifetime of sewing, Debbie began quilting in 2002. She experimented with many different techniques and styles in an effort to figure out what kind of quilter she wanted to be. In 2006, Debbie discovered *The Modern Quilt Workshop* by Weeks Ringle and Bill Kerr, and knew right away that she wanted to make bold, graphic quilts like the ones in the book. Further inspired by the work of Gwen Marston, Jacquie Gering and others in the online modern quilting community, Debbie now describes her style as graphic modern minimalism. Making quilts with clean lines and bold shapes is her focus, whether the colors are deep and intense or low-contrast neutrals and whether the technique is piecing or appliqué.

Debbie's work has been displayed at both Paducah and Houston, and featured in various magazines and books. The main focuses of her work are her pattern business, Esch House Quilts, and sharing her love of modern quilting and appliqué through teaching. Debbie blogs at http://eschhousequilts.com and is active on several social media sites. She is president of the Ann Arbor (MI) Modern Quilt Guild and a member of the Greater Ann Arbor Quilt Guild.

 Published by Fons & Porter Books, a division of F+W Media, Inc., 10151 Carver Road, Suite 200, Blue Ash, Ohio 45242. (800) 289-0963. First Edition.

a content + ecommerce company

www.fwcommunity.com

20 19 18 17 16 5 4 3 2 1

Distributed in Canada by Fraser Direct
100 Armstrong Avenue
Georgetown, ON, Canada L7G 5S4
Tel: (905) 877-4411

Distributed in the U.K. and Europe by F&W MEDIA INTERNATIONAL
Brunel House, Newton Abbot, Devon, TQ12 4PU, England
Tel: (+44) 1626 323200; Fax: (+44) 1626 323319
Email: enquiries@fwmedia.com

Distributed in Australia by Capricorn Link
P.O. Box 704, S. Windsor NSW, 2756 Australia
Tel: (02) 4560 1600; Fax: (02) 4577 5288
Email: books@capricornlink.com.au

SRN: T6438
ISBN-13: 978-1-4402-4397-4

Edited by Stephanie White
Design and Photography by Corrie Schaffeld
Production coordinated by Jennifer Bass
Illustrations by Sue Friend

Metric Conversion Chart

To convert	to	multiply by
Inches	Centimeters	2.54
Centimeters	Inches	0.4
Feet	Centimeters	30.5
Centimeters	Feet	0.03
Yards	Meters	0.9
Meters	Yards	1.1

Find more quilting inspiration with Fons & Porter!

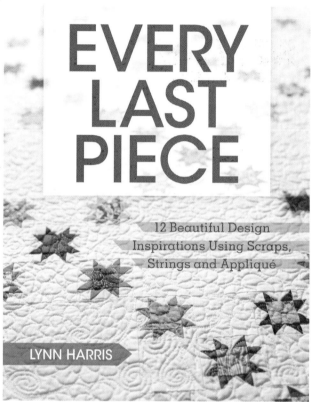

Modern Quilt Perspectives
Thomas Knauer

Every Last Piece
Lynn Harris

In *Modern Quilt Perspectives*, you'll do more than learn the how-tos of making twelve engaging, usable quilts-you'll explore the idea of why you quilt and the meaning behind your personal art. Popular quilt and fabric designer Thomas Knauer leads the conversation, sharing the whys behind these twelve quilts.

Make the most of your stash with these twelve striking quilt designs! Learn to use fabric pieces of every size, from scraps to yardage, in *Every Last Piece*. Author Lynn Harris demonstrates numerous ways to maximize how you use fabric in quilts, including string-pieced blocks, mini star blocks, applique, sawtooth borders and more! Traditional designs are refreshed by giving them a scrappy look. Other quilts use small scraps on broad backgrounds for a minimalist charm.

For more, visit us at fonsandporter.com!